the bathroom makeover book

the
bathroom
makeover
book

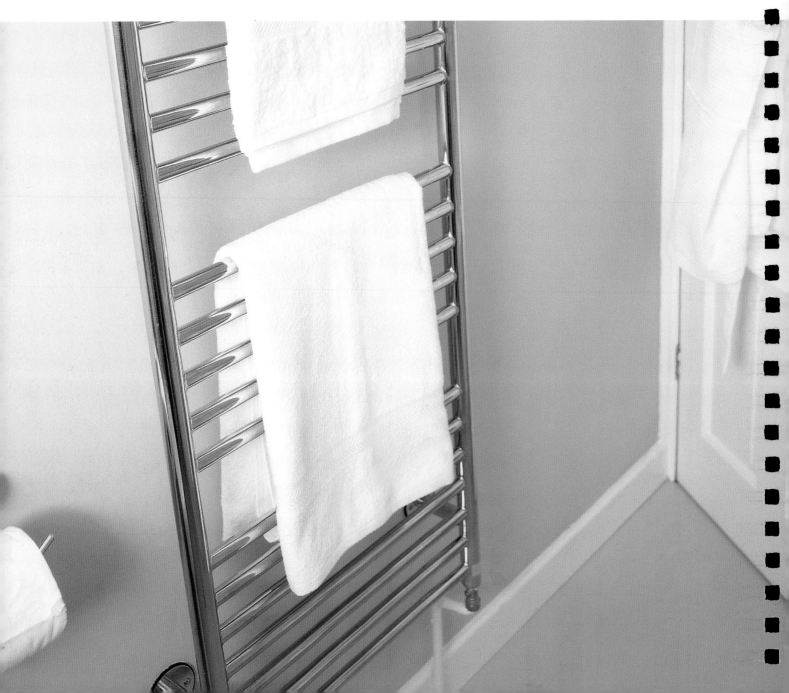

Ideas and inspiration for bathrooms of all shapes and sizes

**Nikki Haslam and
Bernadette Fallon**

hamlyn

First published in Great Britain in 2003 by
Hamlyn, a division of Octopus Publishing Group Ltd
2–4 Heron Quays, London E14 4JP

ISBN 0 600 60742 9

A CIP catalogue record for this book is available
from the British Library

Printed and bound in China

10 9 8 7 6 5 4 3 2 1

In describing all the projects in this book, every care
has been taken to recommend the safest methods
of working. Before starting any task, you should be
confident that you know what you are doing, and
that you know how to use all the equipment safely.
The publishers cannot accept any legal responsibility
or liability for accidents or damage arising from the
use of any items mentioned, or in the carrying out of
any of the projects described.

Measurements Both imperial and metric
measurements have been given throughout this
book. When following instructions, you should
choose to work either in metric or imperial, and
never mix the two.

contents

introduction

Planning and designing a bathroom is one of the biggest challenges the home owner will face. The bathroom is generally one of the busiest rooms in the house, although frequently the smallest and one of the most expensive to fit out. It has to be functional and practical, atmospheric and inviting, and able to cope with both hectic mornings and relaxed weekends.

Whether you want to make a sweeping style statement or simply create a space that is welcoming, safe and efficient, this book has all the information you need to help you make the right decisions. And if you are lacking in inspiration, do not despair. In Chapter Two you will find ten great bathroom looks with lots of hints and tips on recreating them in your own home, plus 20 step-by-step projects.

There is much more, too. From planning the initial layout to choosing the fixtures, creating a design and colour scheme and working out all the practical problems, this book will take you through the various steps involved in pulling it all together.

RIGHT **Getting the layout right is the key to a practical and stylish bathroom, so it is important to spend plenty of time in the planning stages looking at the various options.**

ABOVE **Finishing touches play a major part in achieving a stylish design scheme so take time when choosing taps and accessories.**

The perfect bathroom should be a relaxing haven that functions efficiently, looks good and is a pleasure to use. Regardless of its size, it should offer convenience and comfort and be a private retreat – no matter how many people it caters for. This chapter provides you with all the information you need to begin the decision-making process, as well as giving you plenty of hints and tips to make your bathroom work for you. Whatever the size of your budget you will find plenty to inspire you on the following pages.

planning your bathroom

Planning a bathroom can be a little daunting. It is one of the most expensive rooms to fit out, although often one of the smallest. It is the second busiest room in the house and one of the first and last places you see every day. It must be practical and relaxing, functional and comfortable. The ideal bathroom should create the perfect space in which to indulge both body and mind.

Spatial considerations

Start with the basics. Look at your existing bathroom or the space you plan to allocate to your new one. Look at the position, or the proposed position, of the basic fixtures. If they are squashed together in a cramped space, consider separating certain facilities. Perhaps there is space elsewhere for a small washroom and/or toilet? If you don't have space for a separate shower within the bathroom, think laterally. Is there a redundant airing cupboard or idle recess that could be converted into a shower cubicle? Or consider installing it under the stairs, in a bedroom corner or within a run of built-in wardrobes. Look at the overall facilities for washing throughout the house and ask yourself whether they meet your needs today and, just as importantly, whether

they will still be adequate in a few years' time. Consider dividing a large bedroom to provide an en-suite facility, especially if you are catering for a large family. Or perhaps you could replace a bedroom dressing table with a vanity unit and basin. Consult the experts – a qualified plumber or builder will be able to assess your current situation and advise on the options available to you.

Practical constraints and requirements

Once you have considered all the possibilities, you need to look closely at the room as it stands. If you are renovating an existing bathroom, the most important thing to consider is the layout of existing water pipes, sewage outlets and ventilation ducts. This will determine how much scope you have in moving your fixtures to free up more space or to style a whole new interior. Take advice on local water and building regulations before making any major plans. If moving fixtures is an option, try to keep the main elements close to their original supplies to minimize the restructuring costs involved.

If you are planning to install new fixtures such as a power shower or spa bath you need to consider whether your current plumbing system can cope with the new demands. Decide whether you want a bath or shower, or whether it is possible to fit both. An over-bath shower is always a good space-saving compromise. If you are considering fitting additional fixtures such as a bidet or an extra basin, again a professional will be able to advise on your options.

Look at your heating requirements and existing lighting. Will you opt for central heating or use a separate room heater? Is your lighting adequate for shaving and applying make-up, as well as for soothing relaxation when bathing? How much natural light is there? If you cannot redesign your whole lighting scheme, a simple change such as adding a dimmer switch outside the room or perhaps just a few candles might do the job.

On a practical level you need to ask yourself whether your wall and floor surfaces are suitable for a hot steamy bathroom environment and whether you have adequate ventilation. Finally, pay attention to the finer details such as storage, taps, accessories and other finishing touches. Make sure you have adequate space to store all the items a busy bathroom requires. Remember that the right taps will complete the perfect picture, the wrong ones will jar and look out of place. Make sure decorative touches like stylish light pulls and useful accessories such as soap dishes, toilet roll holders, towel hooks and toothbrush mugs tie in with your overall look, and that you have allocated enough space near the relevant fixtures for them.

LEFT **The ideal bathroom should be practical and efficient, as well as relaxing and indulgent.**

Once all the essentials are in, will you have enough space left over to hang paintings and photographs, or display ornaments or collectibles? Bear in mind the time given over to contemplation in this room and don't stint on creating a space that offers visual stimulation and beauty.

Setting a budget

The first thing to do is to set yourself a budget and stick to it! Don't forget to include installation and decorating costs. Consider extras in the budget that you might not have thought of, such as plugs, waste traps, cistern handle, taps, mixers, light pull, thermostats, pumps and plumbing parts. If you have to make a large outlay on fixtures and plumbing you may find you have very little left when it comes to the final stages of decorating. Don't overlook the finishing touches such as toothbrush holder, waste bin, bathmat and towels.

Start planning

The planning is the most important part! Get it right before you begin the work – it will save a lot of trouble and stress in the later stages.

Start by creating a mood board. Take inspiration from magazines, books and catalogues and tear out pictures of styles that appeal to you. Gather favourite paint swatches and fabric samples and stick them on a large sheet of cardboard along with the pictures. This will help condense all your ideas and give you a visual plan for how you would like your room to look.

Once you have a clear picture of the look you are aiming for, it is time to get out there and see what is available. Visit local bathroom showrooms and study sample displays for ideas. Look at catalogues and check out what is on offer online. You will also get useful ideas on layout and finishing touches by visiting show homes on new housing developments. Spend plenty of time looking around before you buy.

Then, once you have decided on a plan of attack, get costs for the fixtures, installation and decorating, ensuring of course it is within the constraints of your budget. Get a few quotations – in writing – from professional bathroom installers. Three quotes should be enough to allow you to make an informed – and economical – decision. Always ask for references, and follow them up. If possible, take personal recommendations when hiring plumbers, electricians, tilers and glaziers, or contact the relevant trade or technical association for a list of its members in your area. Always confirm the arrangements in writing, establish how long the job is likely to take and what services are likely to be out of action and for how long, so that you can plan alternative facilities. If you have only one bathroom, being without it for even a day can be extremely inconvenient.

Take advice from specialist associations and trade organizations. National organizations for home improvements will help you make contact with trade federations and are a good source of general advice.

ABOVE **Make sure your accessories tie in with the overall look of your bathroom and that you have allocated enough space near the relevant fixtures for them.**

assessing your lifestyle & needs

A bathroom will be different things to different people. A large family will obviously make more extreme demands on the space than a single householder. A bathroom used mainly by the elderly or young children will involve radically different styling from a room that is used only by a young couple. Planning your bathroom involves assessing your lifestyle, needs and demands – both as they are currently and as they are likely to evolve over the years. It is necessary to ask yourself a few key questions before you start, to help plan the most effective space for *you*.

ABOVE **Planning your bathroom involves assessing your lifestyle, needs and demands – both as they are currently and as they are likely to evolve over the years.**

Who will be using the room?

Look at issues such as the number of people using the bathroom and how often. If you are catering for the demands of a large family whose members will all need the bathroom at the same time, consider installing additional fixtures like a second basin or a bidet to provide additional washing facilities which can be used simultaneously. Think about replacing an over-bath shower with a separate shower enclosure, or installing showering facilities and vanity units elsewhere in the house. You should also consider these adaptations if styling a bathroom for a busy couple who may both need it at the same time.

Consider whether the facilities are suitable for all the family. A step up to the bath is ideal for small children, and also useful for a parent when bathing babies or toddlers. Think about height restrictions and safety – small children may bang their heads on low basins, and tall people will hate bending over low fixtures.

If elderly people will be the main users of the space think about installing a special low-sided bath or shower. Elderly or less-able people will also benefit from a higher toilet or raised toilet seat. Consider your choice of taps, too – lever-operated fittings will be easier for them to use.

If the bathroom will be used primarily by the very young or the very old, you need to pay close attention to safety features such as slip-resistant flooring, thermostatic shower mixers and anti-scald valves. Grab rails at key points in the bathroom such as near the bath, in the shower and next to the toilet are also a good idea.

Carefully consider the needs of those who will be using the space and think about what you expect from a bathroom. Are speed and efficiency the most important criteria? Are relaxation and recuperation the crucial ingredients? Or perhaps it is essential to have both at different times, and create a space that is a sanctuary as much as a utility.

What type of fixtures?

Take time to consider your choice of fixtures, flooring and wall covering. If children will be using the bathroom, make sure the materials you choose are child friendly. Remember that some materials need more cleaning than others. Lots of pretty bottles and lotions around basins and baths may create an eye-catching display but may not be practical if they are within reach of small children. What are your priorities? Style at all costs, or a hard-wearing, low-maintenance environment?

What type of look do you want?

Deciding on the type of look for your new bathroom can be tricky as there are so many different schemes to choose from. Your mood board (see page 11) should help point you in the right direction.

Be creative with styles. If you cannot afford an authentic Victorian roll top bath or a stainless steel bathroom suite, create a period or contemporary look with accessories and with fittings like taps and light pulls.

When choosing colour schemes and fixtures, think carefully about how easy they will be to live with. Be careful about going for an ultra-modern suite, brightly coloured tiles or weird and wacky fixtures – you may love them now but for how long? Neutral tiles and classic shaped suites are ideal for working into future schemes – a few new accessories and a fresh colour on the walls can give you a totally different look without the expense of retiling or a new bathroom suite.

RIGHT **A hydro bath with invigorating spa jets and a built-in seat is a luxury option, but if you consider it a long-term investment that will benefit every member of the family, it does not seem so extravagant.**

choosing your suite

Getting the suite right is an important element in putting together a bathroom that looks good and performs well. Baths, basins, toilets and showers are expensive purchases, so you need to get it right first time to avoid living with costly mistakes. You will also need to consider hidden extras such as taps and handles for a style-conscious bathroom that does an effective job.

Getting ideas

There is a huge amount of choice available, but don't be frightened or put off by the bewildering range on offer. Gather all the information you need by looking at books, magazines, bathroom catalogues and websites – and don't forget you may be able to e-mail your queries direct to the experts online.

Buying a matching suite is the easiest and quickest way to get your desired look. But remember you can also mix and match separate pieces to create your own individual style. Make sure when selecting individual pieces that you use complementary styles so that the look you end up with is consistent.

Visit as many showrooms as you can and don't be afraid to ask questions or look for suggestions. Take a carefully planned approach:

- **Do your research**
- **Shop around**
- **Ask for advice**
- **Take your time**
- **Weigh up all the options before you buy**

In the next few pages you will find an introductory guide to choosing each key element of your suite, whether it is a power shower or a luxury bath, a wall-hung basin or a contemporary bidet. Find out about all the options available, discover what you should look for and consider the key questions you should be asking before making your choices.

ABOVE **Buy a matching suite for convenience, or mix and match pieces for an individual look.**

ABOVE **Choose individual pieces carefully to fit in with the overall look. An under-countertop basin gives a sleek finish.**

RIGHT **Shower cubicles range from the most basic units to luxury hydro-massage designs incorporating body jets, built-in lighting, ambient sounds, a radio and a clock.**

baths

Few things are more relaxing than a long hot bath at the end of the day. Your choice of bath will be dictated by space and budget constraints, but with so many options available, neither should be allowed to limit your imagination.

The choices

A vast array of bath shapes, styles, materials and sizes are in today's showrooms. Don't be embarrassed – get in and try out your bath for size and comfort before you buy!

- **Acrylic baths** offer the widest range of choices as they come in a variety of shapes, sizes and colours. Lightweight, warm and affordable, the most sturdy option is a reinforced model with a rigid well-insulated finish.

- **Roll top baths** add a touch of 'old world' luxury to a bathroom. Cast iron originals are robust and durable, but very heavy; reproduction fibreglass models are considerably lighter and more affordable.

- A **composite bath** is made from a combination of materials and is stronger and more durable than acrylic, as well as scratch resistant.

- A **porcelain** or **vitreous enamelled steel bath** is both rigid and tough, but has a colder surface than acrylic.

- Choose **stainless steel** for a contemporary look, or splash out on a **stone bath** – smooth, heavy and dramatic but extremely expensive!

- For the ultimate luxurious experience invest in a **whirlpool** or **spa bath**.

LEFT **A circular bath will make a real style statement in a large, contemporary bathroom and is a must-have for indulgent, luxurious bathing.**

ABOVE **Roll top baths work equally well in both contemporary or traditional settings. Their exteriors can often be painted in any colour to tie in with your scheme.**

Design

Buy as big a bath as you can afford and have the space for – you will never regret it. Be clever when making your choices. If you have a particularly small bathroom, look for space-saving models with tapered ends to fit into awkward shapes, or for a shorter-than-average bath with an integral raised seat to stop you bumping your toes. A corner bath will leave valuable wall space free for other fixtures or storage. It may also be a more practical choice for an awkwardly shaped room. If shopping for two, a double-ended bath allows two people to bathe in total comfort – and with a central waste and taps, you won't have to fight over who's getting the uncomfortable end!

get the look

- If you have the space, position your bath on a raised, tiled platform to create an interesting focal point and hide ugly pipework. Or set the bath in the platform to achieve a luxurious sunken effect.
- A step up to a high bath is ideal for small children, and also useful for parents when bathing babies or toddlers.
- Paint or stain wooden bath panels to complement your design scheme, or make your own panels using natural wood, suitably waterproofed with a polyurethane varnish or an oil-based paint to finish.

basins

A simple change of basin design will instantly give your bathroom a fresh new look and there are some fantastic shapes and sizes to choose from. Think about swapping a traditional pedestal design for a wall-hung option to free up wall space, or utilize space more efficiently by containing an existing basin in a vanity unit for extra storage. Choose the shape and size carefully to suit your bathroom, and accessorize with stylish taps that complete the look. If you have the space, consider installing two basins side by side, particularly in a busy family bathroom.

The choices

Keep it traditional with a vitreous china basin, or create a strong style statement with a glass, steel or chrome alternative.

• The traditional **pedestal basin** is a popular choice. The basin is fixed to the wall and the pillar base is both a support and a neat way of concealing water pipes and waste outlet.

• The **half- or semi-pedestal** is a variation on the full-length stand that gives easy access underneath for laying flooring and for cleaning.

• If basin height is an issue, opt for a **wall-hung model** that can be fixed at any height. Pipes can be neatly concealed behind the wall, but make sure the wall is a load-bearing one. Think about encasing the lower part of the basin in a contemporary chrome or steel frame and provide space for hanging towels, face cloths and wash bags.

• Installing a basin in a **vanity unit** also allows you to select your own height, with the added advantage of storage and increased surface space for soaps, shampoos, toiletries and shaving gear. The basin can be inset in the unit with the rim standing out from the surface, or semi-inset with the back half of the basin set in the unit and the front protruding for easy access. Integrated basins are crafted as part of the countertop for a streamlined look and easy cleaning.

• An **under-countertop basin** is a stylish twist on a traditional vanity unit design, integrated just below the counter for a streamlined seamless look.

Buying tips

■ Think of the long-term consequences when making your choice of basin material. Fashionable surfaces may not wear well and will need extra cleaning to stay in tip-top condition. Sealed stone and wooden basins are tactile and elegant, but will push up costs and need extra attention. Consider the effect of small children and smeary fingers when you make your selection.

■ Check that the tap holes are where you want them when buying your basin.

Design

Whether you opt for trend-setting glass or traditional china, wall hung or pedestal mounted, give careful attention to the final design of your basin. It should be as large as space allows, deep enough from front to back to enable you to bend over without banging your head on the wall, and set at a comfortable height. The front lip should not be so wide that you strain your back bending over it. The most practical designs have space for washing items around the edge.

Taps should be sited well back and should project as little as possible over the basin edge. If you prefer wall-mounted taps, ensure they will not get in the way when bending over the basin.

LEFT If you're choosing a basin for a small bathroom, think carefully about storage. Look for styles that have special built-in shelves for toothbrushes, soaps and shaving gear.

ABOVE An under-countertop basin like this one is the ideal choice if you want a sleek, streamlined look. A specially designed cupboard underneath provides plenty of storage.

toilets and bidets

Gone are the days of the solely clinical and functional – design is now the key when making your selection from the wide range of toilet fixtures on offer. Opt for a streamlined model that looks good and fits unobtrusively into the space available. And if you don't have one already, consider installing a bidet which is an excellent additional washing facility.

The choices

Most toilet bowls are made from glazed vitreous china and come in a range of designs so there are a number of factors to consider when making your choice. Should the cistern be hidden or in view? Do you want a wall-hung or floor-standing model? Consider what will best suit your needs and the space available.

- Traditionally, cisterns are **close coupled** to the pan, sitting either directly above or connected by the flush pipe.

- A discreet alternative is the **back-to-wall** model where the cistern is concealed behind a wall or fitted furniture for a streamlined effect with the pan standing directly against the wall or furniture. This gives a neat uncluttered effect, ideal for a small bathroom. If you are building a false wall to enclose the cistern, extend the sides out to provide a semi-recess between the original wall and the false wall. If you cut out a panel in the false wall and fit a sliding door then you can create useful storage for a toilet brush and toilet rolls.

- If space is tight, look at the **corner cisterns** and toilets on the market.

- A **wall-hung** model offers a clean minimal look. The cistern is again hidden from view and the pan juts out from the wall above the floor. It has the advantage of allowing you to set the pan at the height of your choice, and leaves the floor area clear for easy cleaning and a streamlined uncluttered effect. Do ensure the supporting wall is strong enough to take the weight of the structure – and the person on it!

Design

Toilet seats come in a range of styles and finishes. Standard choices are moulded plastic or wood composite; for a slightly more luxurious option choose from natural woods such as teak, mahogany or pine. Wraparound lids provide a sleek finish, but if you are after something a

bit more funky, there is a huge range of fun coloured seats available, enclosing everything from fish to flowers within plastic casing. Cistern handles are traditionally side or front mounted, but can be button-style set into the top of the cistern or discreetly into the wall behind. The flushing action must comply with legislative water regulations. Dual flushes, which consume standard or smaller amounts of water depending on requirements, are environmentally friendly options.

Add a bidet

If you have the space, a bidet is an excellent addition to the washing facilities in your home and is particularly useful for small children and elderly people who may have difficulty getting in and out of the bath. Essentially a low-level wash basin, it uses very little water and is ideal for a quick freshen up. Usually made from vitreous china in a range of styles to match other fixtures, bidets can be floor standing or wall hung, tap filled or supplied with water from under the brim.

ABOVE **When installing a bidet, make sure the positioning is comfortable and that you have allowed ample room at the sides for manoeuvre.**

ABOVE **A cistern-mounted button flush and neat streamlined shape creates a very continental look.**

LEFT **This style of toilet works particularly well in traditional, period or country bathroom schemes and can be useful if space is very tight.**

showers

Nothing sets you up for the day like an invigorating shower and by using on average only one-fifth of the water of a bath you can feel good about doing your bit for the environment too. Whether you opt for an over-bath model or a separate enclosure, a shower is now a must-have bathroom feature.

ABOVE **A corner shower cubicle is economical on space and comes in a range of styles and finishes.**

The choices

Essentially there are three different shower types to consider.

• The most basic is a **mixer shower** with manual or thermostatic controls.

• A **power shower** is similar to a mixer shower but uses an electric pump to boost the water flow rate – essential if your home has low water pressure. A thermostatically controlled model automatically adjusts the balance of hot and cold water flowing through the showerhead as other taps in the house are turned on and off. It is essential for ensuring that you are not frozen or, more importantly, scalded, when showering, and is crucial in a home where children and elderly people use the showering facilities.

• For instant hot showers at any time an **electric shower** is ideal. This heats cold water from the mains as it passes through the unit, and is both economical and convenient.

Design

If space is limited, a configuration that fits snugly into a corner of the room is probably the best option. Ready-made shower cubicles come in a range of sizes, styles and finishes. Luxury models even have integral seats, heated towel rails and soap shelves. Shower panels and doors are available unframed or framed in a range of finishes, in frosted, clear or decorative toughened glass and acrylic to suit any design scheme. An outward-opening door gives full access to the enclosure but an inward-opening door is ideal if room space is limited. Folding, sliding or pivot doors are also economical space savers, and can look very attractive.

If building your own enclosure, ensure that the walls, ceiling and floor are waterproofed by not skimping on the linings, and using the best adhesive you can afford for the tiles. Use a waterproof grout and waterproof adhesive when tiling the shower enclosure. Joints should be sealed with an impervious grout or an epoxy type. Joints between tiles and shower trays should be sealed with silicone sealant. Ensure that your glass panels are made from toughened safety glass and are a minimum of 4mm (⅙in) thick. 4mm (⅙in) glass should always be framed, thicker glass may be left unframed. Check that the door sits well inside the frame when closed to prevent any water leaking.

get the look

■ If you are lucky enough to have the luxury of a large space, spoil yourself with a walk-in wet room, a dedicated shower area with fully tiled surfaces and a drain in the floor.

Shower trays are most commonly made of vitreous china, plastic or ceramic and come in many shapes. Careful installation is required so that the tray does not flex when under pressure and cause leakage. It is a good idea to have your shower tray fitted professionally to ensure that it is level and firmly installed. Some trays have an upstand around the edge, designed to fit under ceramic tiles to ensure a watertight seal. Many trays have a special non-slip surface for safety, but it is worth installing grab handles for stability, especially if the shower is to be used by older people. A fold-down shower seat is a useful extra. Ideal for the elderly, it also saves one-legged hopping when washing feet!

If space is severely limited you will have to consider placing your shower over the bath, and using a shower panel, folding door or curtain to shield the room from splashes and to provide privacy. This option requires a bath that is as wide and flat bottomed as possible, preferably with a dimpled non-slip surface.

Buying tips

- **Hand-held showerheads are generally a more suitable choice for children and the elderly. Spray patterns vary – choose either invigorating needle jets, a powerful single stream or a soft aerated spray.**
- **A shower screen is more effective than a curtain for containing water spray and is essential with a power shower.**
- **If you have a power shower choose a shower tray with a large waste outlet so that the water can drain away quickly.**

BELOW **Over-bath showers are an excellent choice when you are short on space and don't have room for a freestanding shower. To avoid splashes, there's a vast array of shower screens and curtains available to suit any scheme.**

taps and fittings

Taps should not be an afterthought. A chic tap can make all the difference to a suite, so spend some time choosing the style and finish to achieve the right effect and create a sleek, cohesive scheme in your new-look bathroom.

The choices

As with all fixtures you need to consider both looks and practicalities. Do your taps need to be child friendly and/or kind to arthritic hands? Would wall-mounted taps look better in your design scheme? What type of finish most appeals and how will this match your styling? Do you want period or contemporary effects, modern pop-up wastes or old-fashioned plugs? The basic choices include traditional pillar taps, a single mixer tap or a modern monobloc.

- **Pillar taps** comprise a pair of hot and cold taps. Pillar taps with cross-head handles are an authentic traditional choice for a bathroom with period appeal.

- A three-hole mixer comprising a **single mixer tap** with hot and cold handles is another option.

LEFT **Pillar taps with cross-head handles will suit a traditional bathroom.**

RIGHT **A modern monobloc mixer is a sleek contemporary option.**

- The modern **monobloc** option is where a single lever controls the hot and cold action through one mixer tap. Before buying mixer taps have a plumber check your water pressure as they will only work well if the pressure in both hot and cold water supplies is almost equal.

- For up-to-the-minute style and convenience, **electronic radar taps** automatically switch on once movement is detected towards the fittings.

- **Wall-mounted taps** free up space around your bath or basin, unlike the more traditional coupling of taps and fixtures.

Design

On a practical level, chunky handles are generally easier for children or elderly people to manage. If turning taps is likely to be a problem, opt for lever taps that require only a gentle push to turn on or off. A sleek monobloc mixer blends sharp contemporary appeal with a highly convenient design as it can be operated with just one hand to easily control temperature.

Most taps are made of brass, although plastic-bodied models are cheaper – and less durable – options. Choose your finish carefully. Shiny chrome is a traditional favourite, but if your bathroom is used by more children than adults your taps may not be shiny very often. Brass taps look more authentic with some period schemes such as classic Victorian or country themes. Brushed, matt and satin finishes are modern, subtle and relatively easy to keep clean. For a hint of classic opulence, stylish mixed finishes offer a combination of silver and gold.

Waste fittings

This functional fitting has decorative implications that should not be overlooked. The most basic choice is between a traditional plug-and-chain fitting or the more modern pop-up alternative.

RIGHT **For the design conscious, taps set into a wall behind the basin are a quirky but stylish choice.**

choosing flooring, walls & lights

Once you have chosen your bathroom suite, you will want to make sure you show it off to best advantage with the right flooring, wall coverings and lighting scheme. Your final selection will depend on a range of criteria, but your choices should be hard-wearing, stylish and long lasting... and of course safe for all the family to use.

Floors

Flooring is one of the most basic requirements of any bathroom and it is vital to choose a non-slip option as the combination of shiny surfaces and water is a dangerous one. Flooring can also be used to create a particular style or set a mood, and with so many practical and style considerations at stake, some careful planning is called for.

Walls

Wall covering can be as basic or ornate as you like, again there are a lot of options to consider when making your choice. Make sure your final selection sits easily with the overall style of the room.

Light

Lighting must conform to strict safety standards as well as look good in your design scheme, and should work hard to ensure your bathroom is efficient and functional.

Making decisions

Choices must be made based on the merits of each separate feature but before you make your final selection ensure that all elements are complementary and work together to create a practical stylish space.

The following pages take you through all the alternatives – from the conventional to the unusual, and from the traditional to the ultra-modern – so that you can choose your features fully informed.

ABOVE **Flooring can be used to create a style or set a mood but should also be non-slip and practical in wet areas.**

ABOVE **Don't feel you have to conform to the norm. A panelled wall is an interesting alternative to tiles and can be just as practical with proper care.**

RIGHT **Take time when considering your flooring, wallcovering and lighting schemes to ensure that all the elements work together to create a practical but stylish space.**

flooring

Choosing the right floor will depend greatly on the type of bathroom you want, and the people who use it. All flooring options need to be suitable for use in damp, humid conditions, safe even when wet, hygienic and easy to clean. Of course they also need to be attractive to look at, blending with your design and colour scheme.

Each of the following flooring options has its advantages and disadvantages so it is worth taking time to sift through the possibilities and consider all the issues to make a choice that will suit your lifestyle and needs. If your bathroom is a high traffic area used by family and visitors alike, you will need to choose a durable option that is easy to keep clean. If the main users of the room are the very young or the elderly, safety should be your highest priority. Or, if you want to create a haven of luxury and style in your bathroom, you can allow design and appearance to be your key concerns.

Floor tiles

Tiles are a classic and popular choice. They look good, are water-resistant, hard-wearing, long lasting and easy to clean. On the down side they can be hard and cold to the touch, and sometimes slippery when wet. If your budget will stretch to it, consider installing under-floor heating (see page 31) for added comfort, especially on chilly winter mornings. There is an almost bewildering range of floor tiles on the market – so weigh up the options before you buy.

Ceramic tiles can be glazed or unglazed. Glazed are not generally suitable for bathroom floors as they can be very slippery, but unglazed are available with a non-slip profile, making them an ideal choice. Mosaic tiles are small pieces of ceramic tile or glass sold in sheets on a mesh or paper backing for easy laying and are perfect for more contemporary-style bathrooms.

Natural clay tiles like quarry and terracotta have an unglazed surface which looks less clinical than ceramic, and offer good slip resistance in a hard-wearing format. Terracotta tiles may need sealing both before and after laying, so make sure you are aware of this before buying.

Natural stone tiles such as limestone, marble, granite and slate offer varying levels of suitability for bathroom floors. Marble can be quite slippery underfoot whereas slate offers a natural slip-resistant finish but it will need to be treated with a special sealant as it is porous.

LEFT Large floor tiles in a small bathroom help create the illusion of space and provide a clean and streamlined look.

ABOVE **Carpet is by far the most comfortable choice underfoot but it is essential to choose a carpet that is suitable for a damp and steamy bathroom environment.**

Before laying any floor tiles you will need to make adequate preparations, depending on your existing floor surface. Concrete floors must be at least six weeks old and thoroughly dry before fixing ceramic floor tiles. Wooden floors alone are not a good base and must be overlaid with either sealed plywood or plastic sheeting, combined with a flexible adhesive. If your floor is already tiled it is best to remove these before starting again. Consider the weight of your chosen floor tiles when planning an upstairs bathroom. You need to ensure that the ceiling will take the weight of heavy tiles like granite or marble. Check with a builder for safety and peace of mind.

• **Disadvantages:** cold and hard; can be slippery

Carpet

Carpet is the most comfortable choice underfoot and an ideal non-slip option. However, soft pile and water do not mix very well, so choose one that is specially manufactured for bathrooms, rubber-backed and made from cotton or synthetic materials rather than wool. This will be more resistant to a damp atmosphere, although still not ideal for an area that is likely to be continually wet – think carefully before carpeting around a bath used mainly by small children. Avoid permanently fixing a wall-to-wall carpet so that if underfloor pipework needs attention, it can be easily lifted and replaced.

Carpet tiles may be a better option as they can be simply lifted out to dry off or replaced if damaged. They are easier to lay and cut into shape – an important consideration when working in a small bathroom with lots of awkward corners. If you are feeling creative you can also make your own original designs such as borders, checks, stripes and more – let your imagination run wild.

Alternatively, scatter rugs on the floor to enjoy the comfort of carpet without any of the problems.

• **Disadvantages:** not compatible with too much water/damp

Vinyl and linoleum

Vinyl and linoleum, particularly the cushioned varieties, are comfortable, cost-effective, hard-wearing and easy-to-lay options. On the down side they will not suit an uneven floor and may be easily marked and damaged by shoe heels or scuffing.

Modern options come in a range of excellent designs including marbling, wood grain and tile effect for a fraction of the cost of the real thing – if you are working on a tight budget, this is an ideal choice. If you are a keen DIY enthusiast, vinyl and linoleum are easy to lay yourself.

Vinyl and linoleum tiles are useful for awkwardly shaped floors but wide sheets will minimize joint requirements where moisture could seep in causing the floor covering to lift.

For an instant makeover, you can simply paint existing vinyl a different colour for a fresh new look. Make sure that you use a specialist vinyl floor paint.

• **Disadvantages:** easily marked; not suitable for uneven floors

Cork

Comfortable on bare feet and pleasant to look at, cork is both low maintenance and easy to lay. Take care when laying and sealing, however, to ensure it will repel water. Ready-sealed cork tiles coated with a tough acrylic surface are readily available and the most suitable choice. On the downside, cork is more vulnerable to damage from bright sunlight, cuts, cigarettes and household chemicals, so appropriate care should be taken to protect it. Buy it ready-sealed or simply varnish with a floor varnish for a lasting finish.

• **Disadvantages:** easily damaged

Wooden floors and wood-effect laminate

If you are lucky enough to have wooden floorboards, make the most of them by staining, then sealing with a waterproof sealant – they look great in a traditional or country-style room. Thick washable floor rugs in front of baths and basins will soften the look and add colour, comfort and texture to the wood.

LEFT **For something a bit out of the ordinary, use wooden decking squares laid at alternate angles. Seal with a waterproof sealant for a hardwearing, water-resistant finish.**

For a more colourful finish, or to create tiled or stencilled effects, use satinwood paint on the floorboards. Always protect and seal the paintwork with a coat of clear hard-wearing varnish afterwards. Remember that floorboards can be draughty so take this into account when deciding not to cover them.

If you love the look of wood but don't have floorboards, choose wood laminate that is specially designed for use in a bathroom. Never use an ordinary laminate in humid or wet conditions as the laminate will lift and buckle. It is relatively inexpensive and easy to fit, especially if you are fairly confident at DIY. Unfortunately, it can be slippery when wet and care should be taken when laying to ensure a watertight finish around the joints.

• **Disadvantages:** can be draughty and slippery

Natural fibres

Natural fibres such as seagrass, sisal, coir and jute can be vulnerable to damp unless backed with rubber, but are a stylish option if you take proper care. Easy to lay, the natural tones offer warmth and a less clinical appearance than tiles. Some natural fibres can be scratchy and unkind to bare feet so consider texture as well as visual appeal before you buy.

• **Disadvantages:** rough on bare feet; not compatible with water/damp

Rubber

Rubber is a warm, waterproof, practical and – if you opt for one of the many brightly coloured options available – fun choice of flooring. These tiles look brilliant in a contemporary bathroom, especially when two colours are laid in a checked pattern. Special sealants can be purchased which must be used immediately to protect the tiles and prevent marking.

• **Disadvantages:** can scuff if not protected with a special sealer – available from your floor supplier

Underfloor heating Although you may consider it an impossible luxury, underfloor heating can be surprisingly affordable and there is no better way to take the chill off those cold winter mornings when you step out of the shower.

Particularly recommended with cold ceramic tiles, there are a number of choices on the market. Laying electric matting under tiling is a reasonably straightforward option. Alternatively, underfloor pipes can be connected directly to your central heating system. If you don't want to go to the bother of lifting an existing floor, consider installing long low-hung radiators, which hug the skirting board at the base of the wall.

walls

Whether you choose paint, tiles, paper, wooden panelling or a combination of these, essentially you want your bathroom walls to look good and wear well. Consider all the alternatives before making a choice for the best balance of style and practicality.

Wall tiles

Tiling can be an expensive all-over option. If you are on a budget, limit your tiles to areas around the bath, basin and shower. Ceramic tiles are the traditional choice and are available in a wide range of colours, patterns and styles. Alternatively, choose decorative mosaics, timeless limestone or granite, or consider using funky metal, glass, mirror, laminate or clear Perspex screens. However, do be aware of the extra cleaning such fashionable alternatives may merit.

• **Disadvantages:** expensive, can be very clinical and cold

Paint

Paint is is one of the cheapest ways to decorate or quickly update a look. Remember to choose water-resistant paints, designed specifically for use in a bathroom. Oil-based paints with an eggshell or silk finish are best kept for woodwork. Have a go at decorative finishes such as sponging, stippling, ragging or stamping. These are great ways to add interest and texture to your space or hide uneven walls. If you are feeling confident, more complicated techniques such as marbling or wood-graining give a more classic feel. Always remember to seal such paintwork with a matt varnish for a hard-wearing and durable finish.

• **Disadvantages:** not suitable for uneven walls

Wallpaper

Wallpaper can add texture and pattern to what can sometimes be a clinical space. Choose a vinyl paper specially designed for bathrooms, which can be easily wiped clean, or opt for a wallpaper border at ceiling or dado height to soften a painted wall.

• **Disadvantages:** not as damp resistant as other alternatives, not suitable for uneven walls

Wood

Tongue-and-groove panelling is an ideal way to hide ugly pipes and fittings and easily creates a false wall to conceal a cistern. It is inexpensive, fairly easy to fit and works brilliantly in a wide range of styles. Look out for fake panelling which comes in large sheets – its even easier to fit!

• **Disadvantages:** needs to be suitably waterproofed

Tricks with tiles

■ Fit a row of mirrored tiles to a window recess in a dark room to reflect maximum light and create the illusion of space.

■ Remember that large patterned tiles will make a small area seem more cramped, a plain tile will open it up. Create a spacious illusion by laying tiles in a diamond pattern to draw the eye out and make the room seem wider.

■ Opt for neutral colours for long-term viability and future revamps – it is hard to redecorate around a room tiled in red!

■ Never tile over wallpaper, and check for peeling before laying tiles on a painted surface.

■ Plywood is an excellent backing for bathroom tiles as it will not become distorted when wet.

■ Intersperse expensive decorative tiles among less expensive ones to create an attractive effect on a budget.

■ Add splashes of colour with a scattering of mosaics. Embossed tiles are great for adding subtle detail and pattern; profile tiles can be used to pick out features such as mirrors or windows.

■ Paint a few tiles yourself using specialist tile paint to pick up colours in your existing scheme or create a whole new style. Or you can simply enliven plain tiles with coloured grout.

■ Build a wall panel that can be easily unscrewed when boxing in pipes. That way you will not have to break through the tiles to access the plumbing.

ABOVE **Whether you're lucky enough to have a large bathroom or are short on space, paint is the ideal way to transform a room. You can be as bold or subtle as you prefer with colour and it won't break the bank, even if you are on a tight budget!**

LEFT **Wallpaper is a great choice for any bathroom and there are so many designs and textures available that you are bound to find something suitable whether you're decorating a contemporary or traditional room.**

RIGHT **Mosaic tiles look fantastic in contemporary bathrooms and come in a wide range of colours. Often available in sheets, the individual tiles are mounted on a mesh or paper backing making them quick and easy to fix.**

lighting

Getting the lighting right is crucial in a bathroom. It must be bright enough for grooming, gentle enough for lazing in the bath, safe around water, and should create a bright pleasant atmosphere that shows off your bathroom to its best advantage. Used cleverly, lighting can make small bathrooms seem bigger, add period detail and create a romantic ambience or an efficient functional working area. The key is to build variety into the scheme to allow for as many different moods and tasks as possible.

Planning

Do plan your lighting design carefully to ensure it meets your needs, and don't leave decisions until the last minute. There is often a tendency to overlook lighting but it is essential to plan ahead as wiring will have to be positioned before wall tiles and floor coverings are fixed in place.

Take into account the natural light in the room when planning the design. Is your bathroom flooded with light in the morning? Can you position basins and mirrors near the window to make the most of this? What sort of artificial lighting will you need to supplement it at night and on dark winter mornings? How many light controls do you need and where can they be positioned for comfort and safety?

For best results, ensure that your light source does not work from a single switch. If a complete lighting makeover is not possible, consider a simple change for a dramatic effect. Replace a single ceiling bulb with a track of low voltage spotlights or a conventional light switch with a dimmer switch located outside the room.

Layered lighting

For lighting that changes with your mood and needs, a layered lighting system is best. Set low-voltage recessed downlighters in the ceiling to cast bright pools of light on the surfaces below, and set target lights lower down at specific task points like mirrors and basins.

Remember that a light positioned directly over a mirror can create a very unflattering effect – side lights are a much better option. Use wall-mounted lights with attractive shades to create a period look and reduce glare – mount the lights directly on to the mirror to reflect the light and increase the feeling of space.

LEFT **Set the scene for a long, lazy soak with a selection of scented candles. Lie back, relax and unwind.**

Opt for a continuous lighting strip for an even glow, or go 'Hollywood' with a row of bulbs around the mirror for super bright light, ideal for grooming, shaving and applying make-up.

Spotlights

Wall or ceiling spotlights are excellent when directional lighting is called for – and are ideal over a basin or bath. Position over the head end of a bath to provide the perfect light for reading. A shower cubicle can be attractively lit with a shower-proof ceiling or wall light.

Ambient lighting

For more unusual effects, consider floor-recessed lights if you love a modern look or set lights in low tiling surrounding the bath or vanity unit.

Light oil burners and incense sticks for subtle illumination, to instill a sense of calm and provide soothing scent. Use candles in all their shapes, sizes and colours to add a touch of decadence and instantly create a sensual atmosphere – the perfect light by which to enjoy a long lazy soak at the end of a hard day. Use scented candles for an even more luxurious effect, selecting harmonizing colours to soothe the eye.

Lighting tricks

Bounce lights off tiles or shiny fittings to make a small bathroom look bigger and brighter. Lights reflected in mirrors create a feeling of spaciousness, while for atmospheric, intimate lighting, mirror-reflected candlelight creates the perfect setting. Downlighters shining over a water-filled bath or basin will create attractive rippling patterns on the walls and ceiling.

If you have a central light fitting, remove it and replace it with spotlights flush to the ceiling to make the ceiling look higher and create the illusion of extra space.

Bulbs and switches

Choose your bulbs carefully. Tungsten bulbs give a warm, soft, relaxing glow, and are the nearest light to daylight. Halogen bulbs give a bright concentrated effect and are excellent task lighters – use them for a spotlight effect in an area where a lot of light is required. Harsh fluorescent lighting is not an ideal choice for a bathroom.

Don't overlook light switches and light pulls when making your plans. It is pointless blowing your whole budget on a lavish new lighting scheme operated by a dingy old light pull. Opt for a funky switch to complement a modern bathroom or a gently curved style to suit a softer look. Add period detail or contemporary chic with a flattering light pull handle.

Safety For safety opt for low-voltage lights. Buy high wattage for bright task lighting and use a dimmer switch for a gentle evening glow, but ensure the switch is located outside the bathroom. Seek advice from a qualified electrician to make sure your scheme is safe and in line with official regulations. Always choose fittings that are designed for use in proximity to water.

ABOVE **A wooden venetian blind will allow you to control the amount of natural daylight in your bathroom by adjusting the position of the slats.**

ABOVE **Downlighters work perfectly in sleek contemporary schemes to cast elegant pools of light into the room.**

Natural light

Some bathrooms have no natural light so lighting schemes in these rooms will have to be very carefully planned. If your bathroom does have a window, make the most of the natural light available.

A plain glass window will provide wonderful natural light to lift a small space, but in terms of privacy and practicality it may not be the best option. Go instead for etched, opaque or stained glass. Think about muslin curtains or voiles, stylish louvre blinds or even strategically placed plants to partially screen large plain glass windows. Place a big mirror opposite the window which will serve to instantly double the light and space in the room.

Stylish glass blocks are an excellent alternative to sheet glass windows, creating a well-lit space that does not compromise on privacy and gives the room a great contemporary twist.

If the bathroom does not have a window, consider knocking out part of a wall and replacing it with glass blocks to allow light to filter through from a neighbouring room or hallway.

working with colour

Colour is a powerful tool in any makeover. Used effectively it can make rooms look bigger, increase the impact of light, establish atmosphere, suggest a particular style and set the perfect mood.

Choosing a colour scheme can be a daunting prospect for the uninitiated, but a bathroom is the perfect space to try out your colour ideas as a practice run for working with larger areas. Plan your scheme carefully and don't make any rash decisions – you may have to live with your mistakes for a long time afterwards. If you are really reluctant to experiment, keep shades neutral and introduce colour through accessories, towels, curtains, blinds, floor rugs and the shower curtain.

There is a range of colour schemes to inspire and encourage you on the following pages. Take these as a starting point or simply adapt the look to your own space. Experiment, be adventurous with colour and amaze yourself with the results.

Making colour choices

Colour can create mood and atmosphere, lift a room and increase its size, so it is worth giving it a lot of consideration. Start by taking note of colour combinations that appeal to you and build up a collection of samples – tear pages from magazines, take inspiration from favourite paintings and postcards, visit stately homes and design exhibitions and take away catalogues and brochures to study at home. Look closely at colour schemes in friends' houses, restaurants and bars, and at the colours of nature around you. Think about the colours that always lift your spirits, inspire calm or excite you, and use them to create your chosen mood. Or take inspiration from a focal point in your existing bathroom design – a photo, piece of fabric, favourite perfume bottle, or perhaps even the view from your window.

Create a mood board using paint colours and fabric swatches to build up an effect. Use paint tester pots to try out colours on your walls, examine the effect of changing light on the shades as the day progresses. Be aware that something that looks great during daylight hours can totally change in artificial light in the evening. Add flooring samples to consider the completed effect. Only when you are convinced that you have made the right choices should you invest in your selected colours.

Colour guidelines

Although there are no hard-and-fast rules when it comes to choosing colour, there are a few simple guidelines that will make your life easier when contemplating the vast array of shades on offer:

- **Pale colours** make a room look **larger, darker shades** make it feel **smaller**. As a general rule, using similar tones for all the surfaces and furnishings will make a room feel more spacious. The rule also applies to ceilings. Light colours, with their receding effects, will make the room feel taller; dark 'advancing' colours will make the ceiling feel lower.

- **Natural light** has an impact on the colours chosen. If the natural light is warm, cooler colours may be a good option. If the light is cool, warm colours add cosiness. South-facing rooms receive the purest light for most of the day; north-facing rooms have a colder hue; east- and west-facing rooms experience changing light – the former is bright in the morning and colder in the evening, and vice versa.

- **North-facing** rooms tend to be **darker**, and their cooler light can make cool tones appear even colder. Experiment with warmer shades, or select cool colours with warm undertones to compensate. The yellow-toned light in a south-facing room will make a warm colour scheme more intense.

Primary colours
All colours are derived from the three primary colours, red, yellow and blue.

Tertiary colours
These are the result of combining primary and secondary colours.

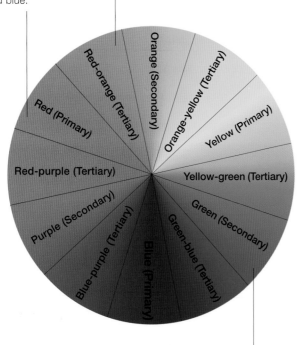

Secondary colours
Mixing the primary colours makes secondary colours purple, green and orange.

The colour wheel

The colour wheel (see opposite) is a useful design tool, which shows the relationship between different colours. There are over two million recognizable colours, all created from the three primary shades of blue, red and yellow.

The cool colours reside on the blue-green side of the wheel. Their receding qualities can make an area seem more spacious. The warm colours on the red, orange and yellow side seem to advance, making a room seem cosy but smaller.

The position of colours on the wheel is an indication of how they will work together. Contrasting schemes combine opposite colour shades for striking effects, harmonious schemes work with colours beside each other, while toning schemes combine several shades of one colour.

• A **contrasting scheme** creates a strong visual impact as it places colours from opposite sides of the colour wheel, for example red and green, beside each other. Choose this contrasting look if you want to create a dramatic effect.

ABOVE **Working with bright colours doesn't have to be daunting. A few splashes, for example a painted wall or the odd accessory, can be just enough to create a colourful, stylish impact in an otherwise neutral bathroom.**

• **Harmonizing schemes** are created by selecting colours that are found next to, or close to, one another on the colour wheel, for example green and yellow. Harmonizing schemes are tranquil and ordered and are great for creating fresh, spacious looks.

• A **toning scheme** works very simply by combining various tones of a single colour, for example royal blue and turquoise, to create an impression of space and light.

The key when combining colours is to select balancing tonal strengths so that one colour does not dominate. Use the colour wheel to help you do this. This works for all your choices, whether wild and adventurous or tried and traditional. For example, delicate pastels always work well together as do bold primaries. But pale tints will be overpowered by vivid colour bursts while muted tones will look flat beside luminous ones.

blue

Blue is a traditional favourite for bathrooms, replicating the nautical look of deep blue seas and the airiness of a fresh summer sky. A relaxing colour, it instills calmness and harmony, making it an ideal choice of colour if you want to create a bathroom with a serene atmosphere.

Successful shades

Pastel blues give the impression of light and spaciousness and can be used to create both traditional and modern looks. A soft cornflower blue is perfect for a retro 1950s scheme dressed up with pretty floral prints, and will look equally good teamed with chrome and beech accessories for a much more contemporary finish.

Be daring with dramatic shades of blue. Rich midnight blue will look great in a classic scheme with a chunky white deco-style suite teamed with classic chrome fittings. Turquoise on the walls will really set off a white suite, creating a fresh, lively colour scheme that is ideal for lovers of all things modern.

If you are looking for a scheme that will not easily date, opt for a palette of muted blues to create a simplistic Shaker-style bathroom.

Colour combinations

- **Shades of blue** Think about combining different tones of blue for a really stylish look. This is an ideal scheme in a tiny bathroom as the colours will all blend together helping to create a feeling of space. Stick to similar tones so that the colour scheme will not jar, and veer towards lighter, brighter shades rather than heavy navys or deep blues.

- **Blue and neutral** If you are drawn to deep blues and turquoise, but are worried they will be too overpowering, use them sparingly with lots of white to create a nautical theme that will look fashionably smart. Or paint one wall in a deep shade to create a focal point and breathe life into a tired bathroom. Alternatively, keep your colours neutral and add your favourite blue through towels, paint trims, accessories and splashes of coloured tiles.

- **Blue and silver** Combine blue and silver for a sleek and modern effect. Paint a recess wall in eye-catching silvery-grey, or dress up a deep blue interior with polished chrome and stainless steel accessories for an up-to-the-minute contemporary look.

- **Blue and green** Pastel blues work particularly well with soft apple greens to create a fairly contemporary look without being too modern.

ABOVE **Liven up a deep blue scheme with some lighter coloured tiles and touches of chrome and silver.**

They are a great combination if you love colour but have a small bathroom and don't want an overpowering effect.

- **Blue and yellow** If you love a Mediterranean look combine a rich cobalt blue with sunny yellow to give your bathroom a summery feel that lasts all year round.

- **Aqua** Light touches of aqua in tiling, paint trim, rugs and towels will lift a deep blue colour scheme and prevent it from looking gloomy and dark. Or use pale aqua as your signature shade and create a dramatic contrast with flashes of a contrasting shade such as vibrant pink or red.

LEFT **A palette of soft muted blues creates a fresh appeal when combined with lots of white.**

LEFT **Highlight key features with a lively splash of colour-coordinated mosaics and create a dramatic effect.**

green

Green is the colour of nature and evokes balance and harmony which will style the perfect relaxing environment. Tranquil and restful, it can be used to create an airy uncluttered atmosphere, and many shades are ideal for a soothing bathroom.

Successful shades

Soft natural greens like willow, sage, herb and moss create classic traditional spaces that do not date quickly. Team them with splashes of white for a fresher finish, or with cream for a more cottagey, cosy feel.

Muted bluey-greens are great for creating period styles such as Art Deco, especially when teamed with sparing splashes of black and white.

If you fancy being bold with colour then be brave and choose strong lime greens to turn your bathroom into a contemporary retreat – but be warned, it is not the most relaxing of colours!

Colour combinations

• **Shades of green** Create a lush and restful haven by combining soft green pastels for a relaxing effect. Or layer lime green with olive for a retro look that is a fresh twist on a traditional scheme.

• **Green and neutrals** Apple green looks stylish and modern when combined with lots of fresh white. For an oriental or more cottagey look mix naturally inspired shades such as sage and willow green with a palette of neutral tones. Natural woven textures work well with a green scheme; add touches of blonde wood for the appearance of lightness and simplicity.

ABOVE **Treat woodwork to a coat of paint in a contrasting shade of green to create a subtle but stylish look.**

• **Green and yellow** Green is an excellent companion for yellow as it brings its restful properties to bear on the brighter shade and opens out the space. Combine sunflower yellow with meadow green to bring the outdoors inside and create a country-style interior. Or team warm yellow with cool citrus green for a sunny effect that is not too overpowering.

• **Green and pink** Go for a traditional look with a soft green and dusky pink colour scheme to create a tranquil space. Or go to the other end of the spectrum and create a bold statement with vibrant lime green and dramatic hot pink.

• **Green and orange** If you are determined to be adventurous, go the whole hog and combine jazzy lime green with fiery orange for an individual look that smacks of confidence but ensure you have the space – and energy – for it!

LEFT **Muted bluey-greens are great for creating period styles. Add a touch of lime for a retro effect.**

yellow

Yellow, the colour of bright sunshine, creates the effect of happiness and light. It lifts the mood and refreshes and stimulates the mind. Warm shades of yellow instantly make a room feel cosier, but beware – when used as the dominant tone it can also make a room seem smaller.

Successful shades

Choose yellows for their warmth and depth and avoid harsh lemons and yellows with a greenish tint. Combine soft buttery pastels to style a bathroom with traditional appeal. Add pretty gingham curtains and towels for a country cottage effect.

Use dazzling sunflower yellow for an ultra-modern look and to bring light flooding into your bathroom.

Mustards and golds will add an opulent touch and create a feeling of warmth and richness, perfect for more traditional or period schemes.

Colour combinations

• **Yellow and blue** Mix sunflower yellow with cobalt blue to give your bathroom a bright Mediterranean feel. For an alternative approach, introduce splashes of blue as an accent colour in a bright yellow colour scheme.

• **Yellow and white** Let your exotic nature take over with rich gold, bright mustard or sun-baked sand, but remember to use sparingly in a small room as it will reduce the feeling of space. It is best mixed with fresh white to give a spacious effect and add contrast and texture.

ABOVE **Soft, buttery yellow and muted blue creates a bathroom with traditional appeal.**

ABOVE **Style a dramatic interior with a palette of rich yellow and deep olive green.**

pink

Pink can be used to create a wide variety of effects and style moods that are radically different depending on exactly which shade you choose.

Successful shades

Use pretty shades of chalky pastels and dusky pink for a soft nostalgic appeal and to create a country look. Be brave and go for deep pinks or hot fuchsias for a dramatic scheme that will make a real style statement.

Colour combinations

• **Shades of pink** Pretty pastel pinks create a soft romantic glow, but don't overdo them or the end result will be sickly. Instead of covering your walls in shades of pastel pink it may be a better idea to introduce tasteful splashes through patterned curtains, blinds, accessories and towels. Opt for chalky smudgy pastel hues for a more natural look or pretty pastel shades for a fashionable retro-style room.

• **Pink and neutrals** A rich vibrant fuchsia will create a modern funky look. Combine with lots of white to make a dramatic statement, or dress up a white background to spectacular effect with shocking pink splashes. If you are wary about the impact of such a vibrant colour in a small bathroom, paint just one wall in the shade and team it with neutrals for a quirky – yet stylish – approach, or add pink accessories. Team pastel pink with off-whites for a scheme that is very easy on the eye. Complete the look with brass-coloured fittings for a nostalgic effect.

• **Pink and green** Combine soft pinks and apple or sage green for a really stylish finish that will work well in country-style or more modern rooms. Hot pinks and lime greens can be used sparingly to make a dramatic impact, but add the colour through accessories rather than fully painted on walls to avoid a discordant effect.

• **Pink and orange** If you dare to be different, team bright pink and vibrant orange for an extrovert look. For bold schemes such as this, add the colour via paint or accessories so that it is easy to change.

LEFT **Choose hot fuchsia for a funky modern scheme – not for the faint-hearted!**

purple

As with pink, use light or dark purples to style radically different looks depending on your preferences. For a contemporary but subtle style choose soft lilacs, and to create more dramatic schemes be brave with rich, deep shades.

Successful shades

Choose rich shades of plum, aubergine and grape to create an exotic boudoir effect that works well particularly in larger bathrooms, livened up with splashes of gold. The colours can look stunning on the walls provided that the room has plenty of natural daylight. Avoid using them in small, dark bathrooms as they will really overpower the room.

Shades of lilac and lavender are easy on the eye and perfect for creating a modern, up-to-the-minute look. They are easy to live with and will really freshen up a room scheme. Use them with splashes of white or cream for a more subtle finish.

Colour combinations

- **Shades of purple** Strong plum, aubergine and grape are highly fashionable, but used unwisely will create a space that is dark, closed in and overpowering. If you simply love these colours, opt for a feature wall in one of these shades and keep the remaining walls and surfaces neutral, creating a rich exotic backdrop for a large, opulent bathroom with a wickedly exotic feel.

- **Lilac and lavender** The cool shades of lilac and lavender are much more workable in a small space. They are a great way to give a bathroom a light modern touch, and you can style a highly contemporary look by adding lots of white and chrome accessories.

- **Purple and green** Mint and apple greens work well with lilacs and lavenders for a look that is fresh, uplifting and very fashionable. If you are determined to go bold – and have the space to get away with it – team deep purple with rich forest green for a striking effect.

ABOVE **For a contemporary, yet pretty, scheme use soft, chalky lilacs with lots of fresh white.**

ABOVE **Use eye-catching striped tiles to liven-up a plain colour scheme and highlight features.**

neutrals

Styling a neutral theme should not be viewed as a failure to use colour. With an imaginative outlook it can be as varied and textured as the most vivid colour palette – and with far less pitfalls.

Neutrals have a softness and lightness and appear very stylish, blending a tranquil touch with an earthy feel. They can be used to create a look that is luxuriously sophisticated or simple and understated.

Successful shades

Choose from a rich and varied colour palette that includes fresh and off-whites, warm creams and beiges, pebble, ivory, buttermilk, eggshell, sand, chalk, mushroom and oatmeal. Consider the underlying tones when creating your palette – neutral shades have cool blue or warm yellow undertones, cream can look warm while white may be cooler.

Colour combinations

If you opt for a neutral colour scheme, avoid ending up with a bland collection of washed-out beiges, or surrounded in floor-to-ceiling magnolia by adding lots of texture and subtle colour contrasts. Do be practical – neutral colours may not be too forgiving of wear and tear so choose washable fabrics and flooring that is easily wiped clean.

- **Textured neutrals** A touch of wicker or dark wood will give the scheme depth. Introduce textures and weaves through natural-coloured loofahs, thick towels, bleached driftwood and knotty floor rugs in harmonious shades. Clear glass jars filled with natural-coloured soaps, pebbles and shells will add texture and a touch of stylish elegance. Use glazed accessories for a hint of sparkle and sheen, or create a splash of colour and liven up the effect with warm terracotta floor tiles.

- **Contrast and warmth** Mix earthy tones with rich red bases like pale terracotta, pebble and mushroom for extra warmth. Add subtle contrast with soft caramel, cinnamon and biscuit-coloured towels and accessories.

- **Pastel whites** Choose white with a soft pastel undertone for the best effect.

ABOVE **Whether you love sleek, minimal contemporary schemes or something a bit more traditional, blending neutral shades and natural textures will result in a winning combination for your bathroom.**

RIGHT **A muted palette of cream looks stunning with touches of wood for a slightly rustic effect.**

ABOVE **For fresh, modern appeal you can't beat an all-white colour scheme.**

unusual colours

If you are feeling adventurous, be bold and experiment with colours that are not traditionally combined. Go back to the colour wheel on page 36 for inspiration – colours that are not usually coupled together sit furthest apart on either side of the primary colour from which they are derived.

Shocking shades

Team cool shades of green with hot reds, or shock the purists with unconventional couplings like orange and plum, or lilac and chocolate. Be brave and mix three or more colours for added effect. Use sharp colour contrasts or unusual shades in a carefully chosen palette to add a note of smart sophistication. Opt for unconventional shades of traditional favourites such as blues and greens to make an impact that is both unexpected and refreshing.

Being adventurous involves a little bit more than just throwing a mix of garish colours on walls, ceiling and floors – a recipe for disaster and a room that will give you a headache. If you are planning a multi-coloured look, make sure your chosen colours are in complementary tones so that one colour does not dominate the others. Use lots of white to prevent the colours jarring or creating a look that is too overpowering. Be clever with accessories like rugs and towels, and use them to draw individual elements of your colour scheme together and present a cohesive style statement.

Touches of colour

If you are unwilling to lose yourself in complete colour indulgence, you can still be adventurous by using colour on door and window frames, floor covering and accessories, while sticking to plain coloured walls and ceiling. Dress up a predominantly white bathroom with vivid splashes of orange, fuchshia or lime green. You will be surprised at the difference bright towels, soaps or ceramic jars will make to an otherwise plain bathroom.

Choose a strong vibrant accent colour to give warmth and depth to a neutral colour scheme. This will also save unnecessary and costly mistakes as the scheme can be easily changed whenever you tire of it. Go one step further and paint a wall, or even just a small section of a wall in a matching shade. While orange or purple walls may scream 'design nightmare' if used on all your walls, floors and ceilings, highlighting just a single wall in one of these shades will make a stylish statement. Dress the room with bold touches such as geometric prints or an unusual piece of sculpture to complete the look and create a highly individual effect.

ABOVE **A bright painted red wall will bring a contemporary-styled bathroom to life. Graphic canvases in contrasting shades will complete the look.**

RIGHT **Bold touches of vivid orange in accessories such as towels and toiletries bring dramatic impact to this turquoise and white scheme.**

BELOW **Keep walls and floors neutral and introduce vibrant splashes of colour in your tiling scheme for an unusual and interesting effect.**

maximizing space and storage

Making the most of your bathroom means using the area effectively as well as clever styling to increase the *impression* of space. Your bathroom has to work hard to meet all your needs, and there are many clever tricks you can use to maximize its space potential.

Storage is a key issue in any bathroom, and the next few pages will take you through all the possibilities. You need to weigh up the options carefully and decide whether you prefer built-in storage or ready-made options, freestanding units or wall-hung alternatives.

There might be underutilized space in the room that could be used more efficiently for storage. Perhaps you could be creative and customize existing fixtures, or do you need to start again from scratch?

Storage facilities should not compromise on style. Adapt your storage needs to your bathroom design to ensure the desired overall effect is maintained. Avoid cluttered shelving and worktops if you are striving for a minimalist look, don't fit out a country or period style bathroom with lots of stainless steel and chrome storage accessories. Work your requirements into your existing design and make storage stylish and attractive as well as practical.

Finally, adapt some of our clever hints and tips on using space wisely to your own particular situation and increase the feeling of space in your bathroom without knocking down any walls!

ABOVE **A sleek wooden towel rail adds a touch of texture to a neutral colour scheme.**

ABOVE **Fit a wall recess with a mirror and glass shelving for stylish space-saving storage.**

RIGHT **A neutral colour scheme combined with a few space-saving ideas can transform even the smallest of bathrooms into a practical yet stylish space.**

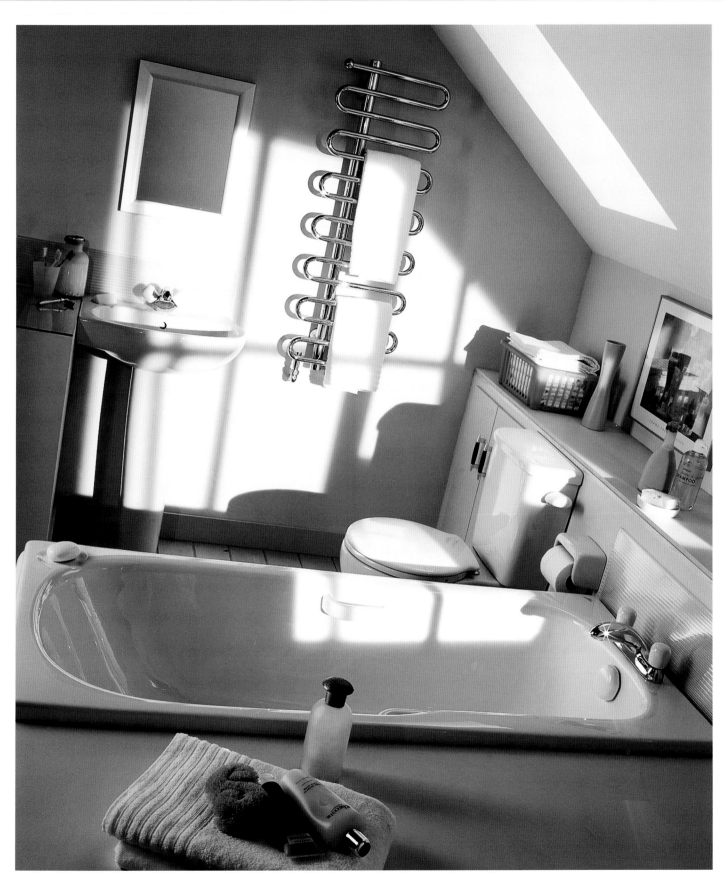

clever storage solutions

When you are planning your bathroom, consider the amount of storage you are going to need. Start by making a list of all the things you wish to keep in the bathroom. Then balance this with the space available and your existing budget.

Storage should not compromise on style. Use storage units, baskets and accessory holders to add texture and colour to a plain bathroom. Choose from rustic wicker, rattan and wood, contemporary metal and steel, funky plastic, stylish glass and china or cool ceramic. There are some fantastic storage products on the market that make clever use of even the smallest space – from towel rails to cabinets and baskets to hanging racks.

Behind closed doors

If you are lucky enough to have room, you can create a feeling of calm spaciousness and keep lines clean and simple by hiding clutter behind closed doors, or make tidy screens by using glass blocks, panelled partitions, slatted blinds or draped voiles. It simply depends on the effect you want and, of course, on the size of the room. Cupboards may look too heavy and dominant in a small space. If so, you could open it up with glass or Perspex shelving.

A large walk-in cupboard is ideal for linen, towels and multi-purpose storage, although few bathrooms have the space to accommodate such a luxury. If you don't have space for any type of cupboard within the confines of your bathroom, think about locating it in the hallway outside. When fitting large cupboards, consider including lights that come on automatically when the doors are opened.

Shelving

If you want attractive bottles and jars, bright towels and stylish soaps and bath toys to add colour, texture and interest to a room, make sure you have lots of display space or open storage containers. Whether you opt for freestanding or wall-mounted, ready-made units or tailor-made options designed to fit into awkward recesses, shelves are the perfect way to create useful storage areas that also look good.

- Glass shelves are stylish, contemporary and look good. Fit them into an alcove and shine a light from above to create interest and impact. If wall space is limited consider mounting them across a window to create extra storage and provide additional privacy. Always use specially constructed toughened glass for safety.

- Wooden shelving is a more practical alternative to glass, as wood requires less cleaning and may be more suitable in a bathroom used mainly by children. Freestanding wooden shelves can look extremely elegant in a bathroom. Stain or paint them in coordinating tones to match your colour scheme or choose contrasting bold shades to add interest and colour. Position tall shelving at a right angle to save on wall space and create an alternative room divider.

- Chrome and steel shelving racks are great contemporary options. A wall-hung chrome rack can be used for multi-purpose storage with the addition of a few chrome kitchen hooks.

- A tiled shelf is another option. If you have the space, don't install your bath flush against the wall. Stand it a tile's width away instead and build a support for a narrow shelf, continuing the wall tiles over it.

- Corner shelves are great space savers – use tiered corner shelving to maximize the space available.

Trolleys

A steel trolley is an interesting alternative to fixed shelving. Group pretty bottles, jars and bowls on top, stack fluffy towels on the shelf beneath. The trolley can be moved freely around to service baths, showers or basins as needed.

LEFT **A narrow, freestanding shelf unit is an ideal option for smaller bathrooms as it takes up minimal floor space. Several shelves provide the perfect place for storing all those towels and toiletries that will otherwise clutter a bathroom.**

LEFT **Mixing closed and open storage with vanity units, glass shelving and a bath rack is the perfect way to create a calm, restful, uncluttered space.**

cabinets, boxes and baskets

For an uncluttered space, cabinets are an ideal choice to keep your bathroom looking tidy. Storage boxes or baskets are another great way to help keep any room shipshape. Use them in cupboards to keep toiletries in order, stack them in a pile on the floor or line them up on open shelves.

Bathroom cabinets

Cabinets with mirrored doors perform a dual function, and those with sliding doors are great space savers for small bathrooms. Invest in a lockable cabinet for storing medicines, cleaning materials or other potentially dangerous items, particularly in a home with children.

Specially manufactured bathroom cabinets come with mirrors, built-in shaver points, fluorescent lighting and even heating units to prevent the mirror from steaming up. Shop around to find the option that best suits your needs. It may be a worthwhile alternative to installing many of the items as separate fittings, particularly if space is limited.

Alternatively, be creative with standard cabinets. Add interest to a plain metal cabinet by decorating the door with tiny mosaic or decorative tiles to create a customized colourful focal point. Or hang two custom-built single wall cabinets side by side to double your storage options, inverting one to create a handy twin unit where the doors open out together like double doors. Liven up existing cabinets and cupboards by hanging new doors incorporating mirrors, trellis-style panels or ornate screenwork.

Storage containers

There are plenty of options for storage containers – from baskets in plastic or natural materials like wicker and sisal to boxes in wood, plastic or metal, either with or without lids.

- Wicker storage baskets are widely available, look great in country-style bathrooms and are perfect for keeping towels tidy. Choose sisal baskets for oriental or more contemporary schemes. Use a large wicker picnic hamper as a rustic alternative to a laundry bin.

- An antique chest is another idea for holding clean towels or dirty laundry and adds a touch of old-world charm. Place it under a window where it can double as a handy window seat. Complete the effect with a throw in rich velvet or cool cotton, casually draped over it for both comfort and style.

- Perspex drawers are a fun and funky storage option for brightly coloured towels and other bathroom accessories. They look good and have the added advantage of transparency so you can locate what you need quickly and efficiently.

- Be creative with unwanted boxes from around the house that might otherwise be thrown away – convert them into stylish bathroom storage options instead. Use old biscuit tins with decorative lids for a shabby chic effect, add a rustic touch with wooden orange boxes, or decorate plain boxes with colour montages and paint effects.

LEFT **In large rooms, stylish bathroom furniture can provide the answer to all your storage problems – from freestanding cupboards to sink units with built-in shelves and towel rails.**

FAR LEFT **Stack sisal storage baskets neatly into a corner of your bathroom to keep piles of towels tidily hidden but always close to hand.**

towel rails and hooks

A towel rail is an essential piece of bathroom equipment and can be as simple or elaborate as space – and taste – dictate. Choose heated rails for warm fluffy towels at any time, a space saving ladder model for small rooms or a simple ring design for pared-down style. Hooks provide lots of useful storage while taking up hardly any space.

Heated towel rails

For pure luxury opt for heated rails, so you can swathe yourself in a warm fluffy towel after a bath or shower. Install a customized radiator with incorporated towel rail, which will look good and heat the room as well as your towels. Clever ladder-style options offer space-saving alternatives that can be hung on the wall over a bath.

Remember though that towel rails heated by your central heating system will not function in summer when the heating is turned off. You might therefore want to consider installing a rail that can be connected to the hot water system or an electrically heated substitute. Bi-functional designs are plumbed into the central heating system but can be switched to electric power when the heating is turned off.

Hanging storage

For a striking and more unusual touch in a spacious traditional or country-style bathroom simply prop an old wooden ladder against the wall to use as a towel rail. It will also provide a useful spot to hang magazines and bathrobes. For a more conventional look, however, there are plenty of other hanging storage options.

- **A row of hooks** or hooks with multiple arms will accommodate more towels than a single towel rod. Hooks attached to the back of a door are great for hanging towels, bathrobes and laundry bags without taking up much room. Hooks on the inside of cupboard doors are another good option. Use them beside a basin for pretty toilet bags and hanging soaps if shelf space is limited.

- **Peg rails** look great in a Shaker-style bathroom and can also be used to hang towels, robes and accessories.

- **Pivoting towel rails** that swing back against the wall are great space savers.

- **Towel rings** in a range of stylish finishes take up very little wall space although they are not as effective for drying towels as a rail.

ABOVE **Sleek, heated towel rails are great space savers – and what could be better than stepping out of the bath or shower to a warm, fluffy towel?**

LEFT **If your bathroom is short on space, look for clever storage solutions like this tapered towel rail that fits easily in tight corners and also looks good.**

increasing the impression of space

Don't worry if you are stuck with a small, cramped bathroom... take inspiration from these handy hints and tips on using your space more effectively and increase the appearance of roominess in your bathroom.

Spatial illusions

• Keep your scheme monochrome. One colour used on walls, windows, blinds and floors will dramatically increase the sense of space – the lighter the tone, the better.

• Maximize space with dual-purpose furniture, reflective surfaces and clever lighting. Look for accessories that work twice as hard, for example towel rails that incorporate soap dishes.

• Use the space above and below fittings. Position shelving and/or cupboards beneath and above basins, around the bath and in the wall space above it. Be creative with shelving units – standing at a right angle projecting into the room they take up less wall space and form effective room dividers.

• Build a solid surround around the bath to provide extra surfaces for toiletries, soaps, candles and other items, and to provide space for built-in shelving or underneath cupboards.

• Fill an empty wall – one with a window if at all possible – with a built-in bench. It provides an ideal place for relaxing on or pampering yourself after a bath. Add a cupboard or shelving unit underneath to create extra storage. If you don't have enough room for a bench, you can still make clever use of an empty corner by installing a shelf that can also be used as a corner seat.

RIGHT Use your space wisely. Choose specially-designed corner fixtures such as cabinets or basins with built-in storage for towels and toiletries underneath.

LEFT A neutral colour scheme will instantly create the illusion of more space, while cleverly shaped baths will fit snugly into tight corners.

• If storage space around the bath and sink is limited, use the walls. Hang a stylish chrome shower caddy from hooks or shower fittings, use a wall-mounted toothbrush holder and soap dish. Check out accessories with suction fittings, which attach easily to tiles or glass.

• Bath racks in a range of materials are ideal for over-bath storage.

• Place colourful plastic or stylish steel baskets on the floor of the shower and group shampoos, shower gels and soaps in them.

• If you have the floor-space, give an old chest of drawers, sideboard or small wardrobe a new lease of life by using it in the bathroom.

Revamp it with paint, woodstain or varnish to match your design scheme – remember to add a moisture-proof finish, such as polyurethane varnish, for long life. Use it to store towels, make-up, cleaning products – to keep the room clutter-free.

• Stitch small squares of voile to a voile panel to make pockets for lightweight storage and drape it over a window or shower rail, or use it as a screen in front of shelving to hide clutter. You can also buy custom-made shower curtains with pockets for storage.

• Use baskets, trays, pretty bowls or glass jars to divide beauty products into easy-access categories such as body lotions and face creams.

bathroom safety

You want your bathroom to be a calm and relaxing haven, but without adequate attention to safety it could turn into a potential disaster zone. With the dangerous combinations of shiny surfaces and hard-edged fixtures, water and electricity, you need to take extreme care at the planning stages.

Be safe!

• Plan your electrical fittings carefully in consultation with a qualified electrician who will be able to advise you on official regulations and requirements. As a general guideline ensure that standard fittings cannot be reached from the bath and that fittings don't come into contact with water. Lightbulbs should be adequately protected from splashes, moisture and steam. Buy specially designed bathroom lights and always use low-voltage fittings.

• Remember that shiny floors become slippery when wet so invest in specially treated non-slip flooring or use mats with non-slip rubber backing to absorb splashes and prevent falls.

ABOVE **Potentially dangerous substances, like medicines and cleaning equipment, should be kept out of reach in a high cupboard or locked away.**

• Try to ensure that baths and showers have ridged or textured surfaces, otherwise use non-slip mats. Hand rails near the bath and shower are useful safety additions.

• Potentially dangerous substances should be locked away or at least kept out of reach, preferably in a high cabinet with a child-proof catch.

• Fit anti-scalding regulator controls or thermostats to maintain an evenly heated water supply at all times. Try to ensure that hot water

ABOVE **Choose fixtures with rounded edges in a small bathroom to minimize the risk of injury if somebody falls against them.**

LEFT **Always make sure that the light fittings you choose for a bathroom are suitable for use in a damp, steamy environment.**

ABOVE **If the bathroom is being used by the elderly or less able, hand rails fitted alongside the toilet, basin and bath are a great idea to aid manoeuvering.**

taps cannot be easily reached by small children. Hot water pipes should be boxed in to prevent accidental burns.

• Think about height restrictions. Small children may bang their heads on low basins. Cabinets and shelving should not be placed directly over a toilet, bidet or bath where they could pose a potential danger to somebody standing up quickly. Also, items could fall from cupboards or shelves and damage fixtures.

• Fixtures with rounded edges are safer than those with sharp corners, particularly in a small bathroom where they may cause injury if somebody falls against them.

• Ensure your bathroom is equipped with adequate ventilation. If steam is allowed to collect it will encourage the growth of mould and mildew. If you don't have a window that opens, you may be legally required to fit an extractor fan.

• Fit door locks that can be opened from the outside in case anybody becomes locked in the bathroom. Alternatively, keep a spare key just outside the door.

Whether you are putting together a look on a budget or are about to throw caution to the wind and style a glittering interior complete with sunken bath and acres of floor space, you will be looking for lots of inspiration and advice. This chapter offers both and has something to suit every personality and taste, with ten great bathroom schemes which can be easily adapted to your own individual space.

makeovers and projects

projects
- storage unit
- mosaic pattern

rhythm and blues bathroom

Bring rhythm and energy to your mornings with this bright, exuberant design. The plain contemporary suite and sleek accessories work together to create a striking space during daylight hours. In the evenings the lights can be dimmed to calm the space and create a perfect relaxing hideaway for quiet bathing and body care.

This is the bathroom for you if:

✔ Your room is large
✔ You have plenty of natural light
✔ You like a tiled floor
✔ You want a high-energy feel
✔ You like a clean, uncluttered bathroom

This is not the bathroom for you if:

✗ You have no natural light
✗ You like traditional or period schemes
✗ You want a calm atmosphere
✗ Your room is an awkward shape
✗ Your room has low or sloped ceilings

- **mood**: Bold, energetic, refreshing
- **good for**: Morning activities, practical efficiency

colour scheme:

- aquamarine
- royal blue
- clean white

variations: Add more white to intensify the sharp crisp feel.

contrast: Use splashes of bright yellows and oranges for a warmer effect.

step-by-step
storage unit

easy

4 hours

storage
solutions

House your less attractive bathroom clutter in a CD storage chest painted to coordinate with your colour scheme and customized with smart handles and legs.

tools & materials

- Ready-to-finish 5-drawer CD storage chest
- Emulsion paint in three colours
- Paintbrush
- Matt acrylic varnish
- Tape measure or ruler and pencil
- Electric drill
- 5 drawer handles
- Screwdriver and screws
- 2 cupboard legs
- 2 mirror plates

❶ Paint the storage chest with three colours of emulsion to match your colour scheme. Leave to dry for at least two hours then apply a coat of matt acrylic varnish. Leave to dry thoroughly.

❷ Using a tape measure or ruler, mark the centre of the back of each drawer. Drill holes for the handles and screw firmly in place. Attach the legs to the two front corners of the chest and fix the unit to the wall using mirror plates.

good idea Use stencils or paint effects to create an alternative decorative look.

step-by-step

advanced

1 day

decorative ideas

mosaic pattern

Create a Mediterranean feel in your bathroom by using a range of blue mosaic tiles in a clever patterned layout that is eye-catching and colourful without being overpowering.

tools & materials

- Mosaic tiles
- Plain white wall tiles (the same size or smaller than the mosaic sheets)
- Graph paper and pencil
- Scissors
- Waterproof tile adhesive
- Spreader
- Tile spacers
- Waterproof tile grout
- Grouting tool
- Sponge

❶ First decide how many mosaic squares you want in relation to the number of white tiles. Plan your design on a piece of graph paper and use this as a guide while you are tiling.

❷ Mosaic tiles come in different sizes and are usually mounted on a sheet of paper or mesh backing. This makes tiling much easier. Measure the dimensions of your plain tiles and cut the required number of mosaic sheets to the same size.

❸ Apply adhesive to a small area of the wall using a special adhesive spreader. This will ensure that exactly the right amount of adhesive is used. Press the first plain tile into position and insert a tile spacer. Using spacers will ensure that the spaces between all the tiles are equal.

❹ Continue applying adhesive and positioning the tiles, inserting a mosaic sheet where required in exactly the same way.

❺ Leave the adhesive to dry according to the manufacturer's instructions, then apply grout to all the spaces between the tiles and the mosaics using a grouting tool. Wipe off any excess with a damp sponge and leave to dry. To finish the job, polish the tiles with a clean, dry coarse cloth.

good idea Alternatively, use plain tiles with a mosaic border for a more subtle effect.

finishing touches

Stylish accessories, rich colour and eye-catching focal points give this bathroom its fresh appeal. The blue-and-white colour scheme creates a fashionable Mediterranean feel. The basic white floor tiles prevent the strong colours from overpowering the space and splash the room with a lively clean sparkle, while the blue walls subtly highlight the shape of the room. A partition wall performs both a screening and decorative function. Satin chrome and glass accessories reflect the rich tones and maintain the fresh, uncluttered approach.

∩ Show it off!

Building square alcoves into a partition wall allows light to filter right through, while providing an attractive display and storage area for pretty toiletries, vases and jars. Line with mosaic tiles for a reflective surface that adds flashes of brightness.

Good for: Separating walls, dark areas.
Variations: Line the alcove with glass, metal or mirrored tiles.

↻ Heating flair

A real 'must-have', this contemporary chrome radiator is a sleek way to store and dry towels – and heat your bathroom at the same time. It is vertically wall hung for space-saving convenience.

Good for: Limited spaces, or in dull or dark rooms.
Variations: A non-heated towel rail is a good alternative if you don't want the bother of connecting the radiator to your heating system.

∩ Weigh it up

Give your bathroom a chic touch with contemporary glass and chrome bathroom scales. Even if you never dare step on them, they make a great-looking accessory!

Good for: Adding interest to a bare corner, creating an eye-catching focal point in a modern bathroom.
Variations: Choose a simpler design to blend with a bathroom with more traditional style.

∩ Decorative tiles

Splash out on a few extra special tiles and mix them in with a white tiling scheme to provide focal points of colour and texture.

Good for: Breaking up large expanses of tiled wall, adding colour to dull areas.

Variations: Use decorative hand-painted tiles or a mosaic of mirrored tiles.

∩ Stylish shelves

Adding a glass shelf to a recessed window is a great way to increase your storage options and create an attractive feature. If you have a plain glass window, fill the shelf with pretty bottles to provide extra privacy. Alternatively, frost the window with a glass etch spray, available from DIY stores. Always use safety glass with ground edges for shelves.

Good for: Large recessed windows, rooms with limited wall space for shelving.

Variations: Place additional shelves higher or lower if space allows or mount shelves across a mirror instead.

ℂ Lights of distinction

To complete the look of your room pay attention to every last detail. Why not choose ultra-modern fittings like this streamlined wall light for a style that is both functional and fashionable.

Good for: Narrow wall spaces, drawing attention to special features.

Variations: Use lights with rounded shades for a softer look.

projects
- colourwashed duckboard
- revamped picture frames

french-style bathroom

Create a refreshing feel in the morning and a calm atmosphere for night-time relaxing with a French-style bathroom that is timelessly elegant. With its Shaker-style panelling, touches of wicker and uncluttered décor, this bathroom oozes charm and classic simplicity. Tranquil and pleasant, it will surely be a welcoming haven, whenever you use it, by day or night.

This is the bathroom for you if:

- ✔ You like bright airy spaces
- ✔ You love fresh colour schemes
- ✔ You prefer simple designs
- ✔ Your room has lots of natural light
- ✔ You like traditional style but with a contemporary twist

This is not the bathroom for you if:

- ✘ You love vibrant colour schemes
- ✘ You have very modern tastes
- ✘ Your room has no natural light
- ✘ You don't like wooden panelling
- ✘ You don't like pastel colours

- **mood**: Restful, calming
- **good for**: Small rooms

colour scheme:

- cream
- pale aqua
- white

variations: Use another pastel tone, like apple green, for an alternative effect.

contrast: Add splashes of bright turquoise to create lively interest.

step-by-step

colourwashed duckboard

easy

2 hours

decorative ideas

Paint a wooden duckboard to match your colour scheme for a fresh and up-to-the-minute look that signals the end of soggy bathmats in your bathroom.

tools & materials

- Old newspaper
- Wooden duckboard
- Fine sandpaper
- Damp cloth
- Emulsion paint
- Paint kettle
- Paintbrush
- Satin acrylic varnish

❶ Lay down sheets of newspaper to protect your floor. Lightly sand the natural wooden duckboard with fine-grade sandpaper to remove any surface finish. Then wipe over with a clean damp cloth to remove any dust and allow to dry.

❷ Mix one part water with one part emulsion in a paint kettle. Using a paintbrush, apply the wash to the wood, working in the direction of the grain. Build up the colour with additional coats if necessary, allowing the paint to dry between applications.

❸ When completely dry, apply at least two coats of satin acrylic varnish for a durable finish, allowing the varnish to dry thoroughly between coats.

good idea Paint a duckboard in a coordinating shade to tie in with your colour scheme, or use bold, contrasting shades to add a bright splash of interest to a bathroom floor. Have a go at spraying the duckboard with metallic paint or glitter paint for a really funky finish.

step-by-step

easy

4 hours

decorative ideas

revamped picture frames

Smarten up old picture frames with a quick lick of paint and some new mounts to coordinate with your colour scheme. Use them to frame favourite pictures or photographs and in no time you have new accessories for your restyled bathroom.

❶ It is important to prepare the surface of the frames carefully so that the new paint finish will look good. Cover the area where you are working with newspaper or an old dust sheet. Remove any existing pictures and the glass from the frames. Using medium-grade sandpaper, sand the frames until you have completely removed any old paint or varnish. Once you have prepared the surfaces, wipe down with a clean, damp cloth to remove any dust and leave to dry thoroughly.

❷ Using a small paintbrush apply a coat of satinwood paint to each frame and leave to dry thoroughly. Once this coat is fully dry, apply a second and leave to dry.

❸ Turn each frame face down and measure the inside dimensions where the mount will sit – the mount will be the same size as the glass. Cut the mounting card to fit using a craft knife on a cutting mat, taking care to cut away from, rather than towards, you.

❹ To cut the aperture for each picture out of the mount, place the mount face down and the picture on top. Mark the position of the corners faintly with a pencil. Lightly join up the marks using a set square to ensure that the lines are perpendicular. Now draw new lines approximately 3mm (⅛in) inside the original ones so that the aperture will be slightly smaller than the picture. Cut along the lines. Stick the picture to the mount with masking tape. Clean and replace the glass, then place the mounted picture on it, and seal the back.

1

2

3

finishing touches

Simplicity and lightness of touch are the key to this design concept. Shades are soft and muted, enhanced by the natural light flooding in through the large window. The subtle floor patterns are picked up by tasteful tile details and softened by the rustic wood panelling. Accessories are contemporary and simple, adding to the feeling of relaxed harmony and calm. The elegant combination of delicate colours and tasteful accessories gives this bathroom a traditional feel with a modern twist.

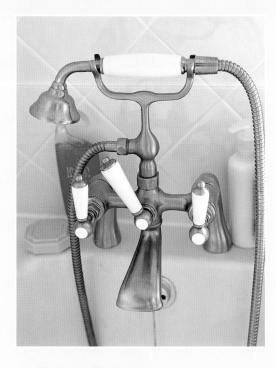

⋂ Retro designs

Complete the look with stylish fittings. This tap and showerhead, with its stylish retro shape and contemporary brushed chrome finish, provides the perfect combination of traditional and modern, essential to this look.

Good for: Creating an eye-catching focal point in a simply styled bathroom.

Variations: Use a brass fitting to create a period look.

⊂ Eye-catching focal point

An old wicker chair can be easily rejuvenated with a coat of satinwood paint, and used to display towels to give country cottage appeal. You don't need to go to the expense of buying new towels to match the room – simply dye them in a colour to coordinate with your design scheme.

Good for: Large bathrooms, clinical spaces that need softening.

Variations: Mix bright contrasting colours, or add a rich throw for warmth.

↻ Chic storage

Customize items from other rooms in the house to create inventive and stylish storage solutions. This chrome pan stand is a clever way of housing and displaying essential accessories.
Good for: Tight corners, small bathrooms where built-in storage is not an option.
Variations: Use a tiered kitchen rack on wheels for bath-side storage and easy mobility.

↻ Blinding success

The key to this scheme is to keep things simple. The gentle drape of this Roman blind in understated natural linen fits the look perfectly. Tasteful and simple, it provides privacy while letting natural light flood into the room, even when lowered.
Good for: Large glass windows, big bathrooms.
Variations: Dress up the look with a floral print or decoratively trimmed blind.

↻ Wooden trims

Use elegant and understated tongue-and-groove panelling around the bath and on the walls to create a fashionable Shaker look or disguise badly plastered walls. Finish with satinwood paint in soft muted shades to tie in with your colour scheme.
Good for: Hiding unsightly walls, boxing off awkward corners.
Variations: Stamp small motifs along the top or bottom of the panelling to create interest.

projects
- window shutters
- romantic coronet

victorian bathroom

Style a look of timeless grandeur to create a bathroom that offers a calm and blissful morning space, as well as a haven in which to relax at the end of the day. A space to engage all the senses, this room is all about pure pleasure. Eye-catching touches like the shutters, a trailing voile curtain and a stylish chair dress up the look and provide tasteful focal points.

This is the bathroom for you if:

- ✔ You are a real romantic
- ✔ You love pastel colour schemes
- ✔ You favour traditional designs
- ✔ You are drawn to 'busy' schemes
- ✔ You like a touch of glamour

This is not the bathroom for you if:

- ✘ You like contemporary schemes
- ✘ You prefer a neutral colour palette
- ✘ Your room is quite small
- ✘ Your favour minimal designs
- ✘ Your room has a sloping ceiling

- **mood**: Luxurious, indulgent, lavish
- **good for**: Large, airy, light spaces

colour scheme:

- lilac
- lavender
- pink

variations: Stick to one pastel tone on the walls for a simpler colour scheme.

contrast: For a more subtle, modern finish, opt for off-white walls.

step-by-step
window shutters

intermediate

6 hours

decorative
ideas

Choose painted shutters to add extra privacy to a bathroom without losing any precious daytime light. They also make a stylish feature out of a plain window and add a nostalgic feel.

❶ Start by painting the doors all over with multi-surface primer and allow to dry.

❷ Next, paint the panels with a coat of purple emulsion. Apply a coat of crackle glaze to the panels, brushing it in the opposite direction to the emulsion paint, and allow to dry for three hours.

❸ Next, apply a coat of specialist kitchen and bathroom paint in lilac – brushing in the opposite direction to the crackle glaze – taking care not to overbrush. As the top-coat dries it will react with the glaze, shrinking back to leave cracks through which the base colour is visible. Paint the door frames with a coat of emulsion in a contrasting shade and allow to dry.

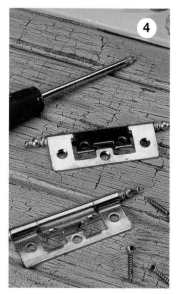

❹ Give the wooden seahorses and seashells a matching crackle finish and glue them to the frame. Finish the shutters by applying a coat of matt acrylic varnish to protect the paintwork. Choose hinges suited to your type of window and attach the shutters to the wall.

good idea Depending on the size of your window, you could use ready-made louvred doors as shutters – simply bring them to life with a lick of paint.

step-by-step

romantic coronet

easy

2 hours

decorative ideas

Enhance the period effect of a roll top bath with an elegant coronet sited above it. Great for a romantic look, it will create a real focal point in the room and is surprisingly simple to make.

tools & materials

- Basketball hoop
- Spirit level and pencil
- Gold spray paint
- Old newspapers
- Electric drill
- Wallplugs

- Screwdriver and screws
- Tape measure
- Scissors
- Voile or muslin
- Needle and cotton
- Pincer-style curtain clips

❶ Holding the basketball hoop in position above the centre of the bath, use a spirit level and pencil to mark the position of the screw holes. Spray the hoop gold using spray paint – always protect the area where you are spraying with plenty of newspaper and spray in a well-ventilated room or preferably outside.

❷ Drill the pre-marked holes in the wall and insert wallplugs. Screw the hoop securely in place.

❸ Measure the distance from the hoop over the edge of the bath and to the floor and add 30cm (12in). Cut two lengths of voile or muslin to this measurement. Hem the top and bottom edges by folding over the raw edge and folding once again, then sew in place. Alternatively, you can use a special iron-on hemming tape and an iron.

❹ Attach the pincer clips to the top of the two voile panels, spacing them evenly along the hem, then clip the fabric to the gold hoop. Drape it neatly over the ends of the bath and allow the excess fabric to gather in a pile on the floor.

good idea Try using a patterned fabric or drape panels of different coloured voile from the hoop to create a sumptuous, layered look.

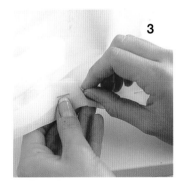

3

4

finishing touches

A Victorian-style bathroom suite creates a comfortable, traditional look that can be updated with the latest soft pastel colours. The exterior of a lightweight reproduction bath is painted with satinwood or acrylic eggshell paint to blend in with the theme, while white paint on the skirting boards and woodwork gives the individual shades clarity. Gently draping voiles, dainty accessories and delicate floral arrangements combine to give the room a soft, feminine touch.

∩ Distinctive flooring

Choose laminate flooring with care as conventional options can swell when wet. Go for wood-effect vinyl planks, which are available in a range of colours, with self-adhesive backing for easy laying.

Good for: Brightening up a small space.

Variations: Paint floorboards with specialist floor paint for an extra splash of colour.

∩ Cool cabinets

Dress up a plain bathroom cabinet and add a hint of nostalgia with flowers, seashells and other decorative objects. A mirrored surface will reflect pretty accessories for a charming effect.

Good for: Over-basin storage, breaking up a large expanse of dull wall.

Variations: Stain the cabinet with wood dye or use satinwood paint to introduce a further touch of colour.

∩ Sparkling touches

Give your bathroom a touch of glamour with luxurious gold fittings. The ideal way to create a period feel, they will liven up a soft pastel colour scheme with a radiant sparkle.

Good for: Victorian-style fixtures, glamorous bathrooms.

Variations: Give the look a more modern feel with chrome or satin finish fittings.

☾ Stage a bath

Raise a Victorian roll top bath on a tiled platform to create an attractive feature, make a practical wet area and hide ugly pipework. Scatter colourful rugs on the floor to provide a soft landing for bare feet.

Good for: Large bathrooms, creating intimate spaces in large and cold areas.

Variations: Use cork or carpet tiles for a warmer finish.

☊ Creative seating

Look outdoors for inspiration. Give a folding garden chair a fashionable makeover with a pearlized spray paint. Add a simple cushion made from two face cloths and a cushion pad. Stitch a lavender bag to the cushion to keep the room smelling fresh.

Good for: Small bathrooms, as the chair can be folded away when not required.

Variations: You can also use it to stack towels or hold toiletries.

☾ Tile themes

Bring the seashore into your bathroom by using delicately coloured tiles with shell, seahorse and starfish motifs. Keep to just one or two colours or opt for a mixture of complementary shades.

Good for: Dark corners, feature walls.

Variations: Vary the theme by using tiles with alternative motifs.

projects
- shelf and towel rail
- stained leaded window

art deco bathroom

Enjoy the simple chic of Art Deco style and create a versatile design classic that works well in both old and new homes. Fashionable and smart, the strong symmetrical lines create a pleasing visual effect. Stained glass in subtle hues, a lavishly draped fabric blind, decorative ornaments and plants have all been added to soften the effect. It is a relaxing bathroom for the style conscious.

This is the bathroom for you if:

✔ You like traditional elegant style
✔ You have a large bathroom
✔ You like a tiled floor
✔ You prefer a muted colour scheme
✔ You are drawn to ordered symmetrical spaces

This is not the bathroom for you if:

✘ You have a tiny bathroom
✘ You prefer contemporary designs
✘ You like a soft streamlined look
✘ You like bright or bold colours

- **mood**: Calm, relaxing, semi-formal
- **good for**: Families, relaxed bathing

colour scheme:

- willow green
- sage green
- black

variations: Try two tones of muted blue on the walls instead of green.

contrast: Go for off-white walls for a stronger look.

step-by-step

shelf and towel rail

intermediate

4 hours

storage solutions

Make a feature out of storage boxes, painted to complement your colour scheme and wall mounted for convenience and effect. A chrome wardrobe rail beneath the unit creates a handy towel rail.

tools & materials

- 2 ready-to-finish storage boxes
- Fine sandpaper
- Emulsion paint
- Paintbrush
- Interior and exterior weatherproof paint

- Screwdriver and screws
- 4 mirror plates
- Chrome wardrobe rail
- 2 chrome wardrobe cup hooks

❶ Lightly sand the storage boxes and paint the inside bottom surfaces with emulsion in a colour to match your wall. Paint the other surfaces with weatherproof paint and allow to dry thoroughly. This finish will be hard-wearing and will not deteriorate in humid conditions.

❷ Attach the bases of the boxes to the wall, side by side, using mirror plates. Ensure your chrome rail is long enough to fit across the length of both storage boxes. Screw the chrome cup hooks to the undersides of the boxes and suspend the rail between them.

good idea Fill open shelving with pretty jars and bottles in coordinating colours to dress up the classic black and white theme. Fix chrome or brass hooks inside the unit to provide extra hanging storage space.

step-by-step

intermediate

4 hours

decorative ideas

stained leaded window

Transform a plain glass bathroom window into eye-catching stained glass to provide extra privacy and make a decorative style statement at the same time.

tools & materials

- Leading kit
- Spray adhesive or masking tape
- Craft knife
- Glass paint
- Artist's paintbrush

❶ Clean and dry the window thoroughly on both sides, then attach the paper pattern that comes with the kit to the outside of the glass, using spray adhesive or masking tape. Following the pattern, use a craft knife to cut strips of lead to the required length and smooth into place on the inside of the glass. Use the boning tool provided with the kit to burnish the lead.

❷ Carefully remove the paper pattern from the glass. Squeeze a small amount of glass paint on to the area to be coloured – on the inside of the glass – and use a small paintbrush to spread it out with a stippling movement. Allow to dry thoroughly, according to the manufacturer's instructions. If you require a more intense colour, apply a second coat using the same technique.

good idea Make your own pattern by tracing a favourite image from an art book or postcard, or an authentic period pattern researched from your local library.

finishing touches

The bold contrast of black against white defines this classic style. The chequerboard floor sets a dramatic tone and the theme is continued in the black and white border tiles. The striking black dado rail that tops them ties the individual elements together to make a cohesive style statement. Period colours are used on the walls, the shelving and window blind lighten the look and add a relaxing ambience. Stylish chrome fittings add to the impression of sleek, integrated luxury.

∩ Moving reflections

Opt for a tilting mirror instead of a fixed one for greater flexibility. Make sure you have enough light near it for grooming – remember side-mounted lights create a more flattering effect than a light that is positioned directly above the mirror.

Good for: Small spaces, empty walls.
Variations: Fit a toughened glass shelf directly underneath to hold everyday toiletries.

⟳ Space to shower

Be creative with space and transform a redundant airing cupboard into a useful shower cubicle. Simply tile the walls to match your design scheme, choose stylish chrome fittings and add a shower door.

Good for: Busy family bathrooms.
Variations: If you have enough space, why not create a walk-in wet room with all surfaces fully tiled and a drain in the floor.

↻ Tile style

Create an eye-catching feature within a tiled floor by inserting a matching border in a central position to give the effect of a tile carpet – a simple idea for a stunning effect.

Good for: Breaking up a large expanse of floor tiles, creating interest in a plain room.

Variations: Repeat the effect several times in a large room for a stylish effect or stick to a simple border around the edge of the tiles.

↻ Handy hooks

There is always a towel to hand with this simple wood and chrome wall rail. It is also great for hanging items such as sponges, loofahs and wash bags to keep bath-side clutter tidy and close to hand.

Good for: Livening up wall spaces near baths or showers and keeping clutter at bay.

Variations: Stain the wood in a colour of your choice. Fit a row of single chrome hooks along the wall for an alternative effect.

↻ Dramatic dados

A dado rail instantly gives a room a period feel. Use a pale colour on the wall above the dado rail and a darker one beneath to make the room feel light and airy. Echo the theme with border tiles.

Good for: Creating a dramatic focal point, highlighting key features.

Variations: Use a harmonizing shade to blend in with a scheme or an accent colour to give definition.

projects
- storage seat
- footprint floor

family bathroom

Dare to be different and create a funky themed family room. It will provide a lively start to the day and make bathtime for the kids even more fun. Let your imagination run wild – an eclectic mix of clever styling tricks, bright colours and fun accessories will bring the seaside into your bathroom, and a smile to your face whenever you step inside.

This is the bathroom for you if:

✔ You have young children
✔ You love bright colours
✔ You like themed rooms
✔ You want a practical space
✔ You want a colourful start to your day

This is not the bathroom for you if:

✘ You like minimalist appeal
✘ You prefer uncluttered spaces
✘ You like calming colours
✘ You favour simple clean designs
✘ You don't have children

- **mood:** Cheerful, fun, exuberant
- **good for:** Families with children

colour scheme:

- sunflower
- sky blue
- orange

variations: For a slightly more subtle finish, stick to just two or three colours.

contrast: Keep walls white and add colour through accessories.

step-by-step
storage seat

intermediate

2 hours

storage
solutions

Combine a comfortable place to sit with handy storage space – this versatile and simple-to-make seat is a real must-have for any family bathroom.

tools & materials

- Ready-to-finish toy chest
- Wood dye or emulsion paint
- Paintbrush
- Acrylic varnish
- Screwdriver
- Scissors
- Foam, 5cm (2in) thick
- Hand towel, for covering seat
- Staple gun

❶ Paint the toy chest using a wood dye or a mixture of one part emulsion to two parts water. Allow to dry thoroughly then remove the chest lid by unscrewing the hinges.

❷ To pad the seat, use scissors to cut a piece of foam to the same size as the lid of the chest.

Using the towel as upholstery material, pull it firmly over the foam and lid and secure on the underside, using a staple gun. Reattach the lid to the chest.

good idea Upholster the top of the chest using a cotton twist bathmat instead of a towel.

step-by-step

footprint floor

easy

4 hours

decorative ideas

Liven up a plain cork or wooden floor with quirky designs, cut in sizes, colours and shapes to match your design scheme.

tools & materials

- Pencil
- Thin cardboard
- Scissors or craft knife
- Sticky-backed plastic in assorted colours
- Clean cloth
- Acrylic matt varnish
- Paintbrush

❶ Make a template by drawing a foot shape onto thin card. Cut out carefully using a craft knife or sharp pair of scissors.

❷ Place the template on to the paper backing side of the sticky-backed plastic and draw around it with a pencil. Cut out with the scissors or craft knife. Repeat this, using different colours if you wish, until you have enough shapes to cover the floor area.

❸ Position the shapes on the floor, ensuring they are evenly spaced. One by one, remove the backing paper and press the feet

shapes into position, smoothing over with a clean cloth to remove any air bubbles. Continue until all the shapes are stuck down.

❹ To protect and waterproof the shapes, paint the floor with two coats of acrylic varnish, leaving the varnish to dry thoroughly between coats.

good idea Cluster shapes around fixtures to create interest at the base of sinks and freestanding storage units, or make a 'path' from door to bathtub using carefully staggered footprints.

finishing touches

Colour and clutter are the driving forces behind this busy, fun family bathroom. The beach hut shower, colourful sea stickers, funky footprints and marine accessories all contribute to the seaside theme. The bright yellow walls guarantee year-round sunshine, with eye-catching splashes of colour added via a bright blind, curtains, towels, shelving and tiles. A lively clutter of accessories and toiletries dominate the wall and floor spaces. The cork floor tiles in a neutral shade show off the bright surroundings to best effect and are guaranteed to be warm and comfortable underfoot.

⋂ Cabinet style

Make a feature of a plain wooden bathroom cabinet by giving it a bright colourwash and attaching some funky accessories. The top of the cabinet can be used as a small shelf for extra display.

Good for: Small bathrooms, themed spaces.

Variations: Stamp or stencil an all-over motif pattern for an eye-catching effect.

↻ Sticky fish

Stickers are a quick and easy way to decorate virtually any surface and can be peeled off at a later date if you get bored with them. Get the kids involved and customize shower doors, bath panels and sink surrounds.

Good for: Plain dull surfaces, adding colour.

Variations: Stickers are available in all colours, shapes and sizes to blend with almost any theme.

⋂ Simple curtains

Create a pair of instant curtains by attaching two towels to a length of tension wire with bright clothes pegs. If you cannot find the right colour towels, try dyeing white ones with a washing machine dye.

Good for: Livening up a plain window, warming a cold space.

Variations: Use patterned towels or stripy fabric for a funky look.

∩ Shelving style

For an unusual twist, fix tongue-and-groove panelling horizontally to the walls to create a brilliant beach hut effect. Add extra interest with simple wooden display shelves, painted in bright contrasting colours, screwed directly into the panelling.
Good for: Extra storage options, brightening an empty wall.
Variations: Display your favourite holiday snaps, shells and other accessories to tie in with the theme.

∩ Colour underfoot

Add warmth and texture with a thick colourful rug. Choose shades carefully to draw individual elements of your colour scheme together.
Good for: Plain floors, cold bathrooms.
Variations: Try dyeing plain white bathmats to tie in with your colour scheme.

∁ Vibrant tiles

Bright ceramic tiles around the bath, basin and shower will really get you in the seaside mood. Go for a combination of vibrant colours arranged in a checked pattern for a lively effect. Finish with coloured grout to complete the look.
Good for: Adding interest and colour to a white bathroom suite.
Variations: Stencil quirky motifs above the tiles to tie in with the look.

projects
- bamboo bathrack
- porthole window

natural bathroom

Create an aura of serenity with this soft natural look, which is a model of clean lines, soothing colours and clever storage. Natural light floods the room from a distinctive feature window, making the bathroom a pleasant space for early morning bathing and grooming. Shiny smooth finishes and reflective surfaces create a contemporary look in a room that will refresh and invigorate.

This is the bathroom for you if:

✔ You love simple spaces
✔ You are drawn to earthy colours
✔ You like natural materials
✔ You prefer contemporary designs
✔ You like a tiled floor

This is not the bathroom for you if:

✘ You like bright colours
✘ You love cosy interiors
✘ You like traditional schemes
✘ You prefer wooden floors
✘ You like a few period details

- **mood**: Calming, relaxing, sophisticated
- **good for**: Style conscious, design lovers

colour scheme:

- stone
- olive green
- cream

variations: Stick to walls in cream and stone colours for a more subtle effect.

contrast: Add more chocolate brown and green accessories for a stronger look.

step-by-step
bamboo bathrack

intermediate

2 hours

storage
solutions

Make your own coordinating accessories for a bathroom full of natural materials. A bamboo bathrack is simple to make and an eye-catching addition to the scheme.

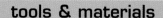

tools & materials

- Thick length of bamboo, plus several thinner garden canes
- Hacksaw
- Electric drill and small wood drill bit
- Hammer and 10mm (⅜ in) panel pins
- Raffia

❶ Take a length of thick bamboo, measuring a little more than twice the width of your bath and cut it in half with a hacksaw so that the lengths fit across the width of the bath, slightly overlapping the edge. Next cut several thinner garden canes into 30cm (12in) lengths. Cut enough to almost fill the length and use them to bridge the gap between the two lengths of bamboo, leaving enough space at each end of the rack for the thicker bamboo to rest on the sides of the bath.

❷ Pin the canes to the bamboo using panel pins. To prevent the canes splitting, drill guide holes first using an electric drill with a small wood drill bit. Turn the rack the right side up. To conceal the panel pins as well as to give the rack extra stability, lash the canes and thick bamboo together using lengths of raffia.

good idea To make the most of your new accessory heap the bathrack with loofahs, natural coloured soaps and cotton face cloths in oatmeal, biscuit or beige colours. Make a matching bamboo ladder on which to hang towels in a similar way.

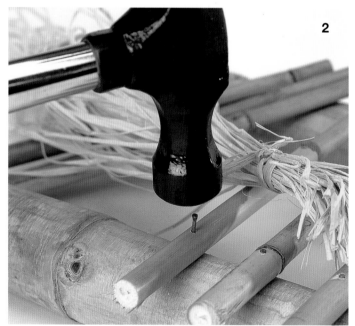

2

step-by-step

advanced

4 hours

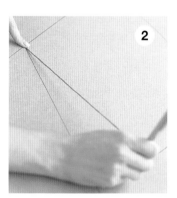

decorative ideas

porthole window

Use this simple but clever trick to disguise an ugly window and make a dramatic style statement. A circular cut-out shape is best for square windows – if you have a rectangular-shaped window, try a rectangular cut-out instead.

- Tape measure and pencil
- Dust mask
- Jigsaw
- 15mm (⅝ in) MDF
- Timber battening (25mm/1in thick)
- Screwdriver and screws

- Pencil and string
- Electric drill and countersink drill bit
- Wood filler
- Paintbrush
- Emulsion paint
- Acrylic varnish

❶ Measure the width and height of the window then, wearing a dust mask, cut the MDF to these dimensions. Cut two timber battens to a length 10mm (⅜ in) shorter than the width of the window. Screw one into the bottom sill and one into the top recess of the window, each 15mm (⅝ in) back from the recess edge so that when the MDF is mounted it will lie flush with the wall.

❷ Find the centre point of the MDF by drawing two diagonal lines from opposite corners. Tie a pencil to a length of string and hold the pencil on the MDF about 20cm (8in) in from one edge. Using your other hand, hold the string taut at the central point. Now slowly move the pencil around the MDF to draw a circle.

❸ On the inside of the circle, drill a large hole close to the pencil line. Put the blade of the jigsaw through the hole and begin cutting carefully around the circle.

❹ Holding the MDF in position against the wooden battens, drill three holes across the top of the panel, through the MDF and into the side of the batten. Repeat on the bottom edge of the panel. Now remove the panel and use a countersink drill bit to countersink the six holes in the panel.

❺ Screw the panel in place in front of the window and fill the countersunk screw holes with wood filler. Apply two coats of emulsion and finish with two coats of acrylic varnish.

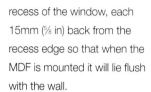

2

3

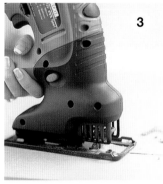

4

finishing touches

Smart contemporary accessories in nature's own colour palette make for an up-to-the-minute look. The combination of natural textures, materials and shades with the cool touch of stainless steel creates a striking effect. Stone and olive green walls give the room a focus and prevent the neutral tones from becoming too bland. Accessories are wall mounted and there are plenty of storage options in place to control and store clutter and provide a fresh, airy space.

◔ Simple style

The simplest items can make an effective design statement when carefully styled. Display an orchid in a stainless steel plant holder to give a bathroom ultra-modern appeal.
Good for: Livening up a dull or dark corner.
Variations: Use additional blooms in bright contrasting shades to add a touch of warmth and colour.

◠ Contemporary storage

Introduce a sharp contemporary note with a stainless steel shelving unit. Add matching steel accessories to complete the effect. Soften the look and add texture with fluffy towels and wicker baskets and ceramic jars to hold toiletries.
Good for: Large plain wall spaces, modern bathrooms.
Variations: Turn the top shelf upside down to form a shallow tray and fill with gravel to make an indoor 'garden'.

☾ Clever mirror

Create the illusion of space by using a strategically placed mirror to reflect light from a window back into the room, making it appear bigger and brighter. Hang or firmly fix the mirror to the wall, or create a similar effect using mirror tiles.

Good for: Small spaces, dark rooms.

Variations: Use two mirrors on facing walls to create the feeling of infinite space.

∩ Stylish panels

Swap a plain old bath panel for a customized wooden surround cut to size. This birch-faced marine plywood blends effortlessly with the neutral palette of a natural-look bathroom. Don't forget to waterproof it with a couple of coats of yacht varnish.

Good for: Providing a streamlined finish, creating a neat space.

Variations: Use different woods to achieve a variety of effects and blend with any design scheme.

∩ Drawer inspiration

Utilize wall space more effectively and keep things tidily to hand with built-in mini drawer units either side of the sink. This is a smart way to reduce clutter in a busy bathroom.

Good for: Limited spaces, breaking up dull areas of plain wall.

Variations: Stamp motifs or letters on the front of each drawer for decorative effect.

funky bathroom

Get your day off to a colourful start every morning with a practical, easy-to-use bathroom that is heavy on style and visual appeal. The vivid shades are perfectly complemented by lots of natural light and pale honey-coloured wood, and the simply styled suite adds a further smart touch.

This is the bathroom for you if:

✔ You have a small room
✔ Your room has sloping ceilings
✔ You like clashing colour schemes
✔ You like wooden floors
✔ You love modern style

This is not the bathroom for you if:

✘ You want a calming space
✘ You don't like bright colours
✘ You prefer traditional schemes
✘ You like a more cluttered, lived-in look
✘ You favour tiled walls

• **mood**: Invigorating, uplifting, energetic
• **good for**: Awkwardly-shaped rooms

colour scheme:

■ bright green   ■ red   ■ white

variations: Choose any two vibrant colours for a similar effect.

contrast: Add splashes of yellow to enhance the vibrant mood.

step-by-step
glass block wall

advanced

2 days

decorative ideas

Build a wall using glass blocks to bring extra light into your bathroom without losing any privacy. It will also create a contemporary and very stylish feature in the room. To determine the overall size of your wall or partition, you need to allow for a 10mm (⅖in) joint of mortar around each glass block.

❶ Ensure the working area is clean and clear of obstructions. Always cover surrounding surfaces to avoid impact damage during construction.

❷ Screw panel anchors to the jambs (vertical edges) and heads (top of the wall), but not to the sill (base of the wall), at 400mm (15¾ in) intervals. The panel anchors will secure the glass block panel to the frame.

❸ Staple or nail foam expansion strips along the jamb (and head if necessary) between the panel anchors to form a cushion between the glass block panel and the wall.

❹ Prepare the mortar mix according to the manufacturer's instructions. Apply a foundation layer of mortar to the sill. There should be a 10mm (⅖in) joint of mortar between the sill and the blocks when they are in place.

❺ Three spacers make up one unit. Trim off different elements to create 'L' and 'T' spacers. Using these 'L' and 'T' spacers on the sill and jamb surfaces, insert the first block at the lower corner. Push the block snugly into place, ensuring that it is properly seated. Place an uncut spacer on the upper corner of the first block.

❻ Apply a layer of mortar to the vertical edge of the next block and put it into place, checking that the block is properly seated. Continue to lay blocks in the same way until you have finished the first course. Periodically check the wall with a spirit level and plumb line to ensure that it is straight, and adjust where necessary.

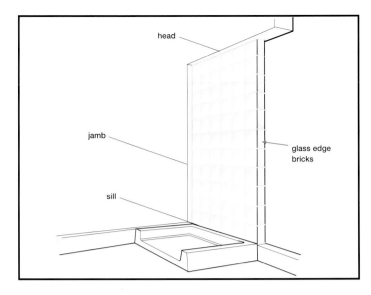

head

jamb

sill

glass edge bricks

7 Make sure that the tops of the blocks, with spacers in place, slip under the panel anchors and apply a layer of mortar to the top of the course, embedding the anchors. Smooth the mortar out and make sure that the crosslegs of the spacers are free of mortar to ensure accurate spacing of the following course. Press a strip of reinforcing rod where necessary (see note opposite) into the mortar.

8 Continue to lay courses, repeating the steps above, until you have completed the wall. When laying the top course, put the 'L' and 'T' spacers in place before inserting the blocks.

9 Use a sponge or damp cloth to remove excess mortar from the faces of the blocks. Rinse often and take care not to use any abrasive products. Do not wait until the mortar has dried. Twist the end tabs off all the spacers.

10 Leave the mortar to set for one hour. Then use a fi round jointing tool to smooth the joints. This will compact the mortar to create a moisture-resistant seal and make your wall look tidy. Once this is done, all the joints should be completely full of mortar.

11 Rake the joints to a depth of 10mm (⅖in). Allow the mortar to set for 24 hours, then fill the joints with panel grout. Wait one or two hours and wipe the block faces clean with a soft cloth.

12 Using a caulk gun, apply silicone sealant continuously along the seams where the glass block panel joins the jambs and head on both sides of the panel.

13 Ensure that the mortar is fully dried and all the inner surfaces are clean before attaching matching glass tiles to the edge of the wall with mortar. If you are building a half-height wall, then attach glass tiles to the final layer of the wall as well.

Important
• Reinforcement rods must be mortared into the top of every horizontal course if you are building a glass panel that spans more than 1.4m (55in) with 190mm x 190mm x 80mm (7½in x 7½in x 3¼in) blocks. If you use more than one reinforcement rod on a course, overlap them by 150mm (6in).
• When building glass blocks into a structured or load bearing wall, a steel or concrete lintel must be placed above the blocks extending into the brickwork on either side by 150mm (6in).
• You must build your wall onto a solid, level base – check with a spirit level for accuracy. Use concrete or cement mortar to level out the base where necessary.
• If the space you are building your wall in does not measure exactly in multiples of 200mm (7¾in), use concrete or cement render to fill the gaps. Create an equal layer on both sides to retain the symmetry; for example, a gap 50mm (2in) too wide will require 25mm (1in) filling on each side before the blocks are laid. Vertical rendering should be built up in layers no more than 12–15mm (½–⅗in). Thick wooden battens (groundings) can be nailed into the wall to ensure the rendering is vertical.
• Never drill or cut the glass blocks.

5

6

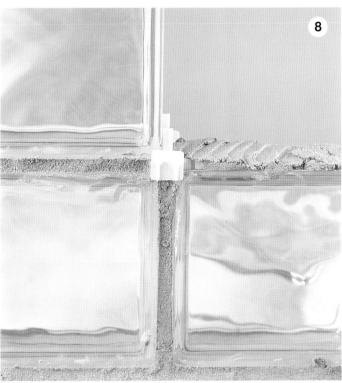

8

finishing touches

Get the look of this bright, modern and funky bathroom with vivid splashes of bold colour, honey-coloured wood, glass blocks and up-to-the-minute accessories. The streamlined wall curves are echoed in the gently curving floor division between wet and dry areas. The rounded fixtures continue the theme while soft rugs and towels provide warmth and harmonizing colour to draw the look together. Striking glass blocks set in the wall behind the bath are a stylish focal point for mini shelves.

⋂ Mirror images

A mirror is a great way of opening up a small bathroom and increasing the feeling of both space and light. You don't necessarily need an empty wall to fit one. Choose a fixture that can be wall mounted straight on to the mirror, such as this basin, for an interesting effect. It is also perfect for all your grooming requirements.
Good for: Small dark bathrooms.
Variations: Use mirrored tiles for a similar alternative effect.

↻ Sexy shelves

Shelves don't have to be boring and practical. Set glass blocks into a plain wall and use as the backdrop for mini floating shelves for a novel approach to bathside storage. Display single false blooms and keep them looking fresh with a quick blast from a cool hairdryer to remove dust.
Good for: Dressing up a plain wall.
Variations: Add longer shelves to increase storage space if you have lots to display.

↻ Dye style

If you already have plain, neutral towels, don't splash out on new ones to tone in with your new look. Instead, simply dye the existing ones to coordinate with your colour scheme. It also saves the bother of tracking down towels in the right shade. Don't hide them away in a cupboard. Arrange them around the room to add splashes of colour, or customize an old wooden chair with a fresh coat of paint in a toning shade and use it to display your new towels.

Good for: Adding colour and interest.

Variations: Dye fabric rugs and face cloths to match.

↻ Separate functions

Use flooring creatively to add interest to the room and mark out separate areas. Here the bathing area has been fitted with a pale wooden laminate to match the honey-coloured wooden bath panel and separate the area from the rest of the bathroom. Ensure you use laminate suitable for use in a bathroom, otherwise it may lift when wet.

Good for: Breaking up an otherwise plain floor, creating a more intimate space.

Variations: Use floor tiles or carpet suitable for bathrooms to achieve a similar effect.

↻ Walls of glass

The sexy curve of this wall has been given a stylish twist by the addition of a row of glass blocks to emphasize its lines and create a stunning visual effect. Glass blocks are a great way of increasing available light in a room, particularly if a window is not an option. If you have a small or dark bathroom consider back-lighting the blocks for added effect.

Good for: Small, dark bathrooms.

Variations: Use mirrored tiles instead of glass blocks for a similar visual effect.

projects

- painted shelf unit
- freestanding fireplace

peaceful bathroom

Calm your senses in this simple, restful bathroom, with its abundance of natural light and uncluttered surfaces. The gently contoured suite with softly scalloped edges creates a harmonious effect while the walls and floorboards are left bare for a look of classic simplicity and pared-down luxury. The room is the perfect haven for morning body care and restful evening bathing.

This is the bathroom for you if:

✔ You favour light airy spaces
✔ You love a neutral colour palette
✔ You want a calming atmosphere
✔ You like an elegant look
✔ You want a timeless look that will not date easily

This is not the bathroom for you if:

✘ You like being bold with colours
✘ You have young children
✘ Your room has no natural light
✘ You like cluttered interiors
✘ You prefer tiled floors

- **mood**: Peaceful, relaxing, calm
- **good for**: Bathrooms of all shapes and sizes

colour scheme:

■ cream ■ off white ■ white

variations: Paint a wall in stone for extra interest.

contrast: Add accessories in your favourite colour for impact.

step-by-step
painted shelf unit

intermediate

6 hours

storage solutions

Give an existing shelf unit a new lease of life with a lick of paint and it will instantly coordinate with your new look. Use it to display a few of your favourite accessories.

tools & materials

- Shelf unit
- Sandpaper or small electric sander
- Damp cloth
- Multi-surface primer
- Emulsion paint
- Paintbrushes
- Acrylic varnish

❶ Start by sanding the shelf unit to remove any existing paint or varnish, using sandpaper or a small electric sander. Wipe down with a clean damp cloth to remove any dust and allow to dry.

❷ Add a coat of multi-surface primer to prepare the surface for painting and leave to dry. Apply a coat of emulsion in an off-white colour and leave to dry thoroughly before applying a second coat.

❸ To protect the finish from scratches and minor damage, apply three coats of acrylic varnish, leaving it to dry thoroughly between coats according to the manufacturer's instructions.

good idea Depending on your style of room you can give an item of furniture a really individual look with stamped or stencilled motifs. Paint the shelf units and apply motifs before varnishing.

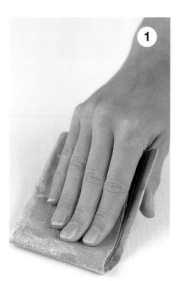

step-by-step

6 hours

storage
solutions

freestanding fireplace

Build a simple freestanding box fireplace in MDF to create a focal point in the bathroom and provide an excellent display area for toiletries, pretty ornaments, candles, glass jars and wicker baskets.

tools & materials

- Tape measure and pencil
- 15mm (⅝ in) MDF
- Dust mask
- Jigsaw
- 19 angle brackets
- Screwdriver

- 12mm (½ in) screws
- Hammer and panel pins
- MDF primer
- Paintbrush
- White emulsion paint
- Matt acrylic varnish

❶ Start by working out the required size of your fireplace, marking the dimensions on the wall using faint pencil lines. Work out the required dimensions of your MDF components. Wearing a dust mask, cut the components to size. You will need two side panels, one top panel, one front panel. For the opening you will need two small side panels and one top panel – all 6cm (2½in) narrower than the main side panels – and one back panel as shown. When working out the dimensions, allow for the 15mm (⅝ in) thickness of the MDF.

❷ Mark out in pencil the fireplace opening on the front panel and cut it out using a jigsaw.

❸ Keeping this panel flat, face down, use three angle brackets to secure one of the side panels in place. Repeat with the other side panel and with the top panel. Now use two more brackets as shown – one each side to secure the top panel to the side panels. This will ensure that the structure is square and solid.

❹ In the same way, secure the three panels that make up the opening to the front panel, using two angle brackets on each edge and a further two to secure the top and side panels together. Now fix the back panel as shown using panel pins to secure.

❺ Turn the fireplace over and apply a coat of MDF primer. Allow to dry, then apply two coats of white emulsion, allowing the first coat to dry before applying the second. Finish off with a coat of matt acrylic varnish to protect the surface and allow the varnish to dry.

❻ Stand the fireplace upright and position it against the wall. If the wall has a skirting board you will need to cut out small sections at the base of the two side panels with a jigsaw, to allow the fireplace to stand flush against the wall.

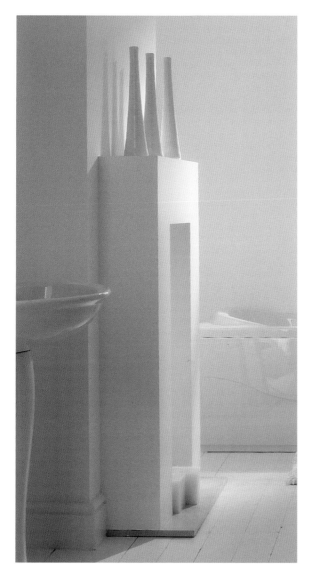

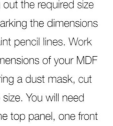

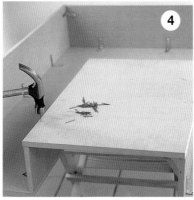

finishing touches

A pale colour palette and unfussy styling creates a simple yet luxurious effect. Warm neutral tones soften the plain walls and floorboards and prevent the look becoming too stark. Piles of fluffy towels in toning shades and a deep pile rug beside the bath add cosiness. Glazed accessories and shiny gold-effect fittings give a touch of sparkle. A few perfectly placed picture frames, a white wooden chair for towels and atmospheric flickering candles complete the stylish picture.

∩ Frame it

Hang a traditional framed mirror over the sink to give the bathroom a touch of grandeur. Strategically placed near a window, it will help reflect light back into the room and create the illusion of space.

Good for: Softening a stark clinical-looking room and increasing the feeling of space.

Variations: Choose an ornate gilt frame for a more opulent effect.

↺ Picture this

Dress up a plain wall with a series of chunky picture frames in matching shades. Fill with pressed flowers, seashells, favourite photographs or quotations for a stylish effect.

Good for: Breaking up large, dull expanses of wall.

Variations: Use slim frames for an effect that is lighter and more subtle.

⟲ Decorative display

Bathrooms can often lack a focal point so an eye-catching fireplace is ideal for breaking up a plain wall. It is surprisingly easy to build and will make a real impact. Fill the recess with large church candles and use the mantle to display a few carefully chosen accessories.

Good for: Adding an interesting focal point in a large room.

Variations: Fit shelves or rails inside to increase the storage options.

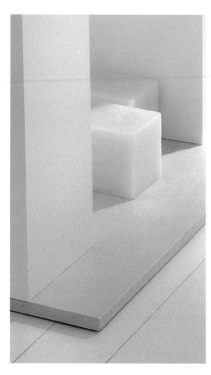

⟲ Catch the light

Shutters are a charming and unusual alternative to a curtain or blind at a bathroom window. They are ideal for plain glass windows and they will allow you to enjoy complete privacy without losing natural light.

Good for: Large plain glass windows, overlooked windows.

Variations: Use a more tightly shuttered or larger panel for greater privacy.

⟲ Stacking system

A narrow space at the end of a bath is the perfect platform for a vertical shelving system. Use it to display eye-catching toiletry bottles, fluffy hand towels and attractive collectibles.

Good for: Small bathrooms, tight spaces.

Variations: Paint the shelves in a contrasting colour to create more of an instant feature.

projects
- painted border
- panelled wall

elegant bathroom

Create a look that is both elegant and glamorous. Tasteful panelling, decorative wood trims, framed prints and recessed shelving combine for a luxurious effect that smacks of sophistication. Stylish, uncluttered and upmarket, this is the ideal bathroom retreat for anyone who is discerning and taste conscious.

This is the bathroom for you if:

- ✔ You love traditional character
- ✔ Your room has lots of natural light
- ✔ You like bold colours
- ✔ You like period details
- ✔ Your room has wooden floors

This is not the bathroom for you if:

- ✘ You like calm colour schemes
- ✘ You prefer modern interiors
- ✘ Your room has little or no natural light
- ✘ You like tiled floors
- ✘ Your room is very small

- **mood**: Grown-up, comforting
- **good for**: Large bathrooms with natural light

colour scheme:

■ cobalt blue   ■ earthy red   ■ white

variations: Use two tones of the same colour on the panels for a striking effect.

contrast: Paint above the dado rail in white or off-white for a fresher look.

step-by-step
painted border

intermediate

2 hours

decorative
ideas

Give a plain bathroom floor a new
focus with a painted border. Make
a real statement with a wide border,
or keep it narrow and subtle for a less
dramatic look.

tools & materials

- Tape measure and pencil
- Low-tack masking tape
- 2.5cm (1in) paintbrush
- Specialist floor paint

❶ First decide on the width of
your border. Using a tape
measure and pencil, measure
10cm (4in) away from the wall
and make a small pencil mark on
the floor. Continue doing this
around the entire room every
20cm (8in) or so, then use low-
tack masking tape to join up the
pencil marks. Press the masking
tape down firmly to ensure that
paint cannot seep beneath it.

❷ Measure from the edge of the
masking tape towards you and
use the pencil to mark the width of
your desired border. Continue
around the room measuring and
marking every 20cm (8in) or so.
Join up the marks with masking
tape as before.

❸ Using a 2.5cm (1in)
paintbrush, start to apply a coat
of specialist floor paint in your
chosen colour between the two
lines of masking tape, carefully
brushing towards the centre of
the two strips of tape to stop the
paint seeping beneath the tape.

❹ Leave to dry and apply a
second coat of paint if necessary.
Very carefully peel away the
masking tape.

good idea Paint different
sections of the floor in different
colours to create added interest
and highlight different areas of
the bathroom.

step-by-step

intermediate

4 hours

panelled wall

decorative
ideas

Attach stylish panelling to bathroom walls for an original touch that will give your room traditional appeal without too much expense. The finished effect is really easy to achieve and looks stunning.

tools & materials	
■ Tape measure and pencil	■ Multi-surface primer
■ Spirit level	■ Paintbrush
■ Wooden moulding	■ Satinwood paint
■ Mitre box and handsaw	■ Emulsion paint suitable for
■ Strong multi-purpose adhesive	bathrooms

❶ Mark where you want the panels on the wall using a tape measure, pencil and spirit level.

❷ Use these measurements to cut lengths of moulding to size. Use a handsaw with a mitre box to ensure that the angle of the cuts is accurate, producing a neat end result when the moulding is fixed to the wall.

❸ Apply a strong multi-purpose adhesive to the back of a piece of moulding and press it firmly into position. Hold in place until the glue becomes tacky. Repeat until your panels are complete.

❹ Prime the mouldings with multi-surface primer and paint with satinwood. Paint the wall and in bathroom emulsion paint.

good idea For a lively effect, paint panels in contrasting colours, and pick up the different tones in towels and other accessories to tie the scheme together.

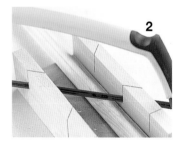

finishing touches

Bold colours in a vivid palette create a look that is classic and smart. Floors are light and natural, with touches of warm wood around the bath and on the toilet seat for a contrasting note. A generously proportioned bath on a raised platform creates interest and adds a touch of luxury. Accessories are kept to a minimum and the shelving is simple and uncluttered.

◑ Floors of distinction

Colourwashing a floor instantly lifts a room and pale colours are an excellent way of creating the illusion of more space in a small bathroom. An understated tramline pattern creates interest in a plain floor and is easily achieved.
Good for: Creating interest in a plain floor.
Variations: Use bright colours to liven up the effect or paint more than one border in different widths.

◑ Bath time

Luxurious dark wood panels give a bath a sophisticated finish and work well with the deep colours of this elegant bathroom. Panels can also be used to create clever storage. Simply hinge one side of the end panel and fit a magnetic catch so it opens like a door while remaining unobtrusive.
Good for: Small rooms with limited storage.
Variations: Fit sliding panels along the side of the bath to access a larger area.

◑ Panelled walls

To create the feeling of an English country house in your bathroom, choose attractive wooden panelling instead of tiles for a warmer, more traditional look. Panelling is a great way of providing flat walls with pattern and definition but must be treated correctly if it is to work well in a wet environment. Cover with paint specially formulated for use in bathrooms – never use ordinary emulsion which will show water marks. Highlight the raised panelled areas in a contrasting colour for an eye-catching effect.
Good for: Creating a cosy, intimate space, adding colour and texture to otherwise plain walls.
Variations: Try the same technique on a plain door or bath panel.

↻ Platform bath

You may think your bathroom is too small for luxurious features such as a raised platform. However, a bath on an elevated floor can work really well, even in a limited space, creating both a focal point and setting the bathing area slightly apart from the rest of the room.

Good for: Breaking up fixtures in a small bathroom, making a feature out of an attractive bath.

Variations: Choose an alternative floor covering for the platform to make it stand out.

↻ Recessed shelving

Make use of alcoves and awkward corners by turning them into useful storage areas. Fit a few deep wooden shelves in a recess and use them to display piles of your best towels, pretty bottles and toiletries.

Good for: Making a useful feature out of awkward corners.

Variations: If you have clutter to hide, fit wooden doors over the shelves to keep it all neatly hidden away.

∩ Framed prints

Pictures and prints don't have to be confined to living rooms and hallways, they can look great in bathrooms, too. Choose carefully so that your pictures work with your existing design scheme. These wooden frames and tasteful prints are offset perfectly by the elegant wall panelling in this bathroom.

Good for: Dressing up plain walls, creating an unusual feature.

Variations: Paint your picture frames to blend in with your design scheme and add a personalized touch.

projects
- simple wood-effect shelves
- mirror frame

zen bathroom

Calm, refreshing and stylish, the theme is light and natural with lots of pale wood, white walls and wide open spaces. The raised platform is a luxurious touch and the perfect way to accommodate a generously proportioned sunken bath. Stones, pebbles, bark and wooden accessories bring the outdoors inside, and create a restful ambience for relaxation and pampering.

This is the bathroom for you if:

- ✔ You have a large room
- ✔ Your room has high ceilings
- ✔ You are drawn to neutral colour schemes
- ✔ You prefer minimal interiors
- ✔ Your room has lots of natural light

This is not the bathroom for you if:

- ✘ Your room is very small
- ✘ You like splashes of colour
- ✘ You have an awkwardly shaped room
- ✘ Your room has limited natural light or small windows
- ✘ You like tiled floors

- **mood**: Calm, luxurious, indulgent
- **good for**: Large, light rooms

colour scheme:

- cream
- stone
- white

variations: Set the bath in a raised platform to create an interesting focal point.

contrast: Add touches of black and willow green to continue the oriental theme.

step-by-step
simple wood-effect shelves

intermediate

2 hours

storage solutions

Increase your storage options by making your own shelves out of MDF to display and store bathroom necessities.

tools & materials

- Tape measure and pencil
- 12mm (½ in) MDF
- Dust mask
- Jigsaw
- Electric drill
- Wallplugs
- Wood glue
- Hammer and panel pins
- Scissors
- Beech-effect sticky-backed plastic
- Small screwdriver and screws

❶ Each shelf consists of five pieces in total. Measure, mark out and, wearing a dust mask, cut to size the following pieces of MDF: two identical pieces, 100 x 70mm (4 x 2¾in), for the sides; one piece, 380 x 124mm (15 x 5in), for the top; two identical pieces, 380 x 70mm (15 x 2¾ in), for the front and back of the shelf.

❷ Holding the back piece against the wall, drill two holes through the MDF and into the wall. Remove the MDF and insert wallplugs into the drilled holes in the wall. Now attach the side, front and top pieces to the back piece using wood glue and panel pins as shown.

❸ Cut a piece of beech-effect sticky-backed plastic 600 x 124mm (24 x 5in). Peel off the adhesive backing and stick across the top and side panels as shown, tucking neatly under the side edges of the shelf to finish off. Gently smooth out any air bubbles using a clean cloth. Cut another piece 380 x 70mm (15 x 2¾ in), peel off the backing and stick carefully on to the front panel of the shelf as before.

❹ Hold the back of the shelf in position against the wall and screw tightly in place using a small screwdriver.

good idea Fix cup hooks to the bottom of the shelf and use for hanging face cloths, wash bags and loofahs. Sticky-backed plastic comes in some great finishes so you can be as bold or subtle as you like to tie in with your room scheme.

2

3

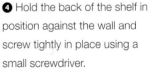

step-by-step

intermediate

2 hours

decorative ideas

mirror frame

Increase the feeling of light and space in your bathroom with a custom-made mirror with the frame stained to suit your colour scheme.

1 Lay the mirror on the sheet of MDF and mark its position with a pencil. Allowing for the width of the wooden frame around the mirror, mark the required dimensions of the MDF backing. Using a jigsaw and wearing a dust mask, cut the MDF to size.

2 Apply a strong multi-purpose adhesive to the back of the mirror and press it firmly on to the centre of the MDF using the pencil marks as a guide. Leave to dry thoroughly.

3 Now measure the length of all four sides of the MDF and cut the planed timber to these lengths, using a mitre box to cut the angled corners accurately. Using wood glue, press each piece firmly in place to create the frame around the mirror and leave to dry thoroughly.

4 Brush woodstain in a colour to suit your room scheme over the wooden frame. Leave to dry. Build up the colour with successive coats until you are happy with the finish, leaving each coat to dry thoroughly before applying the next.

5 Finish by attaching a hanging plate to the back of the mirror. Hang your mirror on the wall in the desired position.

good idea If you are feeling more adventurous, try stencilling the frame for a more decorative effect, or opt for a paint technique such as crackling or dragging for a stylish look.

finishing touches

This spacious room with a sunken bath is a real indulgence. Floor-to-ceiling windows bathe the room in all-day natural light. At night the elegant wooden blinds can be closed, the vast floor space filled with scented candles, and a few plush cushions scattered on the floor for pure luxury. Honey-coloured wood, oatmeal tiles and white walls create a feeling of calm and tranquillity that works effortlessly both day and night. Natural accessories complement the clean, modern, minimalist look and add to the sense of opulence.

◖ The light fantastic

Keep large windows simple and stylish. A calm, minimalist bathroom does not lend itself to fuss and flounces. Keep it clean and fresh with wooden venetian or bamboo-style blinds. Opt for frosted glass if you require extra privacy or if your bathroom is overlooked.

Good for: Large windows, uncluttered spaces.

Variations: If you don't want the expense of replacing your windows, frost them yourself using a special frosting spray.

◑ Streamlined radiator

Don't let ugly fittings jar in a perfectly styled space. There are always stylish alternatives available. This streamlined radiator, for example, will fit perfectly in an alcove to do the job without spoiling the look. Colour coordinate the fitting to tie in tastefully with your design scheme.

Good for: A clean, minimalist bathroom with lots of uncluttered space.

Variations: Hang a heated towel rail as an alternative – it will heat the room as well as providing warm towels!

◖ On display

A platform is the ideal way to create a sense of luxury in your bathroom and is perfect for containing a large sunken bath. It is also an ideal place to display attractive accessories, making it practical as well as appealing.

Good for: Large bathrooms, sunken baths.

Variations: Instead of a sunken bath, use the platform to show off a freestanding roll top bath for an appealing alternative.

∩ Sunken with a twist

A sunken bath is a real luxury and creates a focal point in a large bathroom. For a stylish twist dress it up by filling a sunken floor panel with mixed pebbles and stones at one end of the bath. Complete the look with overhanging twisted willow, a few larger stones and soft fluffy towels.

Good for: Creating interest in a large bathroom.

Variations: Fill large glass vases or wicker baskets with stones and pebbles from a garden centre.

∩ Feature a basin

If your room is large enough, don't clutter your fixtures in one area. Allow yourself the luxury of a whole wall devoted entirely to a basin, a simple framed mirror and a single shelf, and revel in all that space. A streamlined pedestal basin will look best in a large space, so opt for a generously shaped sink with a wide surround for complete comfort. Finish with a single elegant chrome mixer tap for tasteful designer appeal.

Good for: Adding interest to a large plain wall.

Variations: For a busy bathroom, fit a double basin instead.

∩ Textured tile

It is important that a neutral bathroom doesn't become a bland, clinical space. Use tiles to introduce subtle colour hues and make a feature out of a single wall, mixing slight variations in shade to create interest and texture. This will help bring such a neutral bathroom to life.

Good for: Breaking up a large neutral space.

Variations: For a real dash of colour, experiment with bright tiles for an eye-catching splash.

Putting your chosen look together involves careful planning and preparation to make sure the job goes smoothly. Take advice from our helpful tips and hints section, study our sample layouts and use the stickers and grids supplied to get you off to a great start.

putting pen to paper

There is no point coming up with the look of your dreams then finding it will not fit in your bathroom. So, now that you have pulled all your ideas together, selected your fixtures and chosen a colour scheme, it is time to combine ideas with practicalities and plan a layout that looks good and also fits and works in your home.

Follow the step-by-step instructions on pages 126–127 for making a scaled grid plan of your bathroom, then take inspiration from the sample layouts on pages 128–137, designed to tackle bathrooms of all shapes and sizes. While it is unlikely your bathroom will be exactly the same size as those illustrated, you can still use the layouts as a guide. They provide helpful ideas for dealing with the problems that arise from having very little space to work with, having too much space to fill or fitting out an awkwardly shaped bathroom.

LEFT **If you have a small bathroom, look out for streamlined suites, tapered-end or corner baths and showers that have sliding doors.**

ABOVE **Not all bathrooms are regular shapes. If you have an irregularly-shaped bathroom you will need to consider clever design solutions and specially-designed fixtures to make the best of your space.**

Making a scaled grid

Before you knock down a wall, lay a tile or make any major purchases, you need to plan your bathroom on paper using a scaled graph. This will overcome the potential problems of buying a bath that is too big for the space, or finding you cannot actually open the bathroom door once everything has been installed.

How to plan your bathroom

1 Start by measuring each wall of your bathroom. Transfer the dimensions on to the grid supplied (see inside the cover), noting the scale provided.

2 Once you have drawn the outline of your bathroom depicting its size and shape, mark the immovable features of the room – the windows and doors. Remember to allow enough space for opening the door. It is also worth considering whether the door could be rehung to open the other way and give a few extra inches of space.

3 Mark the existing plumbing and electrics, including the layout of water pipes, sewage outlets, ventilation ducts, wiring and light switches on your plan. Mark sloping ceilings if relevant.

4 Decide on your ideal fixtures layout. Manufacturers usually supply exact dimensions of their products in brochures so you can plan each fixture exactly to size. Ensure you allow enough knee and elbow room (see opposite) and space for manoeuvring around each one. Try out several configurations before finalizing your plan.

5 Mark in additional features such as towel rails, storage units, toilet roll holders, shelving and any other fixed items. Make sure you have allowed enough space around cupboards and vanity units for doors and drawers to open fully, and that towel rails and toilet roll holders are within reach of the relevant fixtures. Be sure to allow enough storage near basins and baths for soap, toothbrushes, shampoos, bubble bath and other toiletries.

6 Think about your movements around the room. Ask yourself whether everything is placed conveniently? Is the room easy and comfortable to use? Is it safe? Will it suit all the family? And remember, while large bathrooms may be a luxury, they need just as much planning as smaller ones to work comfortably and look good.

Points to consider

It is important to remember that while sizes are roughly standard when it comes to bathroom suites, there will be slight size differences from style to style and from one manufacturer to another. The fixtures supplied here, in the form of peel-away stickers, are a good guide.

Be aware that certain styles will not work well in some rooms. A chunky Art Deco-style suite is bigger and will take up more room than a streamlined suite. So if you have a tiny room, you will probably have to rule out certain styles of suite, or risk having your room looking overly cluttered and cramped.

Bear in mind that most manufacturers have space-saving alternatives to the standard suites – and again these may vary in size. If space is a problem, look out for baths with tapered ends, smaller-than-average wash basins, narrow toilets and corner fixtures. Consider the following points before finalizing your fixtures layout.

- **The basin:** Make sure there is sufficient space for washing and shaving in comfort with adequate elbow room and enough space to bend over the basin without banging your head on the wall behind, as well as enough space in front for standing comfortably. Allow 80cm (32in) in front of the basin, and 15cm (6in) elbow room either side.

- **The bath:** Allow enough space alongside the bath for getting in and out. If you plan to install a shower over the bath make sure you have sufficient headroom to stand up comfortably while showering.

- **The shower:** Give yourself enough space to step in and out with ease and dry yourself, and allow for an opening shower door if necessary. Allow 70cm (20in) for comfort.

- **Storage and shelving:** Be careful where you fit wall-hung shelving and storage units, particularly when positioning them over baths, toilets and bidets, where somebody standing up quickly could get a nasty bang on the head.

RIGHT **Once you have marked up your bathroom's shape and size on the grid, use the peel-away stickers supplied to try out various configurations of fixtures and fittings that will work in your space and choose the one that works best for you.**

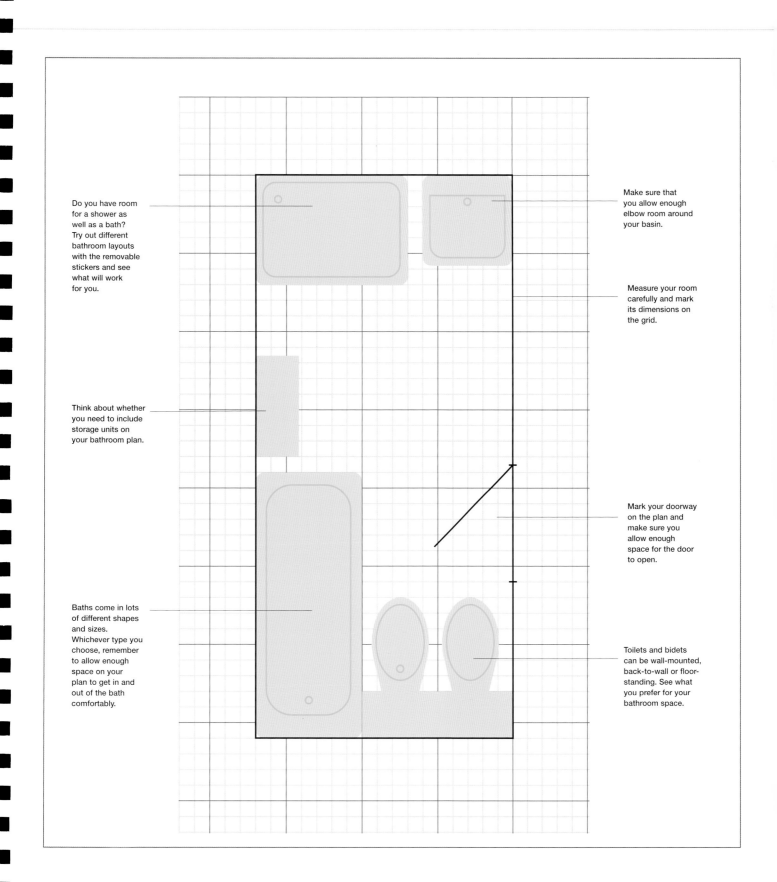

Do you have room for a shower as well as a bath? Try out different bathroom layouts with the removable stickers and see what will work for you.

Think about whether you need to include storage units on your bathroom plan.

Baths come in lots of different shapes and sizes. Whichever type you choose, remember to allow enough space on your plan to get in and out of the bath comfortably.

Make sure that you allow enough elbow room around your basin.

Measure your room carefully and mark its dimensions on the grid.

Mark your doorway on the plan and make sure you allow enough space for the door to open.

Toilets and bidets can be wall-mounted, back-to-wall or floor-standing. See what you prefer for your bathroom space.

tackling different shapes

square bathrooms

ABOVE If you have sufficient space, a freestanding Victorian-style roll top bath will create a stunning focal point and can be painted to tie in with your colour scheme.

A square bathroom poses a unique set of challenges and requires careful planning to avoid looking too 'boxy'. If space is tight, keep the look clean and uncluttered. Avoid overly fussy fittings or too many decorative features, which will intrude on the space and make it seem smaller. Opt for bright colours, and sleek streamlined accessories. Do not mix too many colours, styles or textures – keep the look simple for best effect.

Avoid arranging all the fixtures around the edge of the room when planning the layout for a large bathroom, as this will simply leave a large unattractive, empty gap in the middle. Allow the bath to protrude into the centre space, or invest in a freestanding bath to create a focal point in the centre of the room. Consider grouping certain fixtures together to create a separate washing or storage area. Use movable screens to achieve the same effect and break up the space, creating interest for the eye. You can afford to be bold with colour in a large bathroom. Bold colours also make the walls seem closer, creating a more intimate cosier environment.

Problem 1

This room is quite large but also completely square and in danger of looking clinical and sparse without adequate planning.

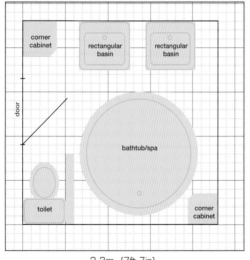

corner cabinet · rectangular basin · rectangular basin · door · bathtub/spa · toilet · corner cabinet

2.3m (7ft 7in)

2.3m (7ft 7in)

Solution

- If you have the space, go for luxury and create a sumptuous and relaxing place in which to bathe. The sunken Jacuzzi is a stunning feature and makes full use of the large central floor space.
- Twin fixtures such as double basins along one wall are another attractive focal point and will alleviate pressure at busy times in the bathroom. Fitting two separate basins gives more flexibility than a standard double unit.
- Freestanding cabinets at diagonally opposite corners of the room give a pleasing symmetry to the bathroom. Fix shelving around the cabinets for extra storage and stylish displays.
- Build a narrow wall along the side of the toilet. Using glass bricks will keep the space bright, create a screened-off area and break up the space.

ABOVE Group dedicated fixtures together in a large square bathroom to create distinctive areas and provide different focal points for the eye.

COLOURS: Make the most of a large bathroom by using sophisticated neutral shades to create a really luxurious retreat.

Problem 2

Here again, the dimensions are quite large and the problem is to create a contained, comfortable room within its parameters.

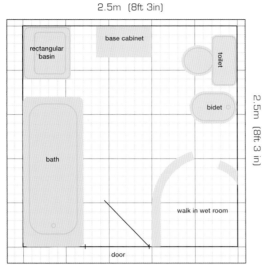

2.5m (8ft 3in)

2.5m (8ft 3in)

rectangular basin

base cabinet

toilet

bidet

bath

walk in wet room

door

Solution

- A dedicated walk-in wet room is a wonderful luxury if space allows and curved shower walls give the angular bathroom a softer look.
- If you have the space for it, invest in a bidet – a great extra washing facility.
- Group the bath and basin together to create a dedicated washing area. Raise the floor slightly on this side of the room if possible – the elevated appearance will create extra visual interest and reduce the boxy effect of the room.
- A large freestanding double cabinet links both sides of the room and provides lots of useful storage.

LEFT If you have a large bathroom it's worth investing in a bidet as a great extra washing facility.

COLOURS: Go for a contemporary look with a Mediterranean twist using vibrant shades of blue with plenty of white for a crisp finish.

Problem 3

This is a very small square bathroom – a typical en-suite – with limited space for fixtures and storage.

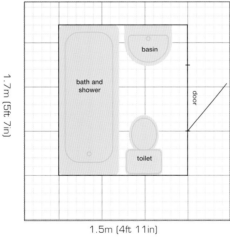

1.7m (5ft 7in)

basin

bath and shower

door

toilet

1.5m (4ft 11in)

Solution

- A bath will fit against the wall opposite the door, and a shower can be placed over the bath. A side screen for the shower also screens the toilet for more privacy.
- A freestanding basin is ideal in a small bathroom. The wall over the basin is a good place for shelves. Choose glass shelving to keep the space light.
- Paint walls in a light colour, and add a mirror or mirrored tiles over the bath to make the room seem bigger. Keep the floor covering in a light colour, and if using tiles, extend them partially up the side of the bath to make the floor area seem larger.

LEFT Less bulky than a vanity unit, a freestanding basin will also expose more of the floor, making the room seem bigger.

COLOURS: Keep walls and floors neutral in a small bathroom and liven up the space with a few towels or accessories in hot pink and purple.

long bathrooms

A long bathroom that is twice as long as it is wide can lead to problems with the room's appearance as well as with possible lack of space. Try some visual tricks to prevent the room from resembling a long and rather dismal corridor.

Be clever with your design scheme during the planning stages. Broad horizontal stripes on the walls, for example, will have the effect of pulling them out to make the space seem wider, so avoid these on the long walls. However, they work well on short end walls to make the room look wider. Walls will look longer if painted in pale, single colours.

Use mirrors on long walls to reflect the room and make it seem wider. Attractive lights, stylish radiators and other decorative features can also be used to break up large expanses of wall and create interest for the eye.

Look at raising floor levels in certain parts of the room to create interest and make the room feel more spacious. Use raised areas for bidets and toilets to give the bath a slightly sunken appearance and create a layered effect, which will serve to draw attention away from the length of the room.

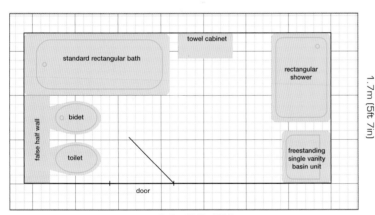

ABOVE Striking black-and-white prints break up large expanses of wall and create interest for the eye in this long Art Deco bathroom.

Problem 1

Although spacious, this room is long and a regular bath will not fit across the width of the room.

towel cabinet

standard rectangular bath

rectangular shower

1.7m (5ft 7in)

false half wall

bidet

toilet

freestanding single vanity basin unit

door

3.6m (11ft 10in)

Solution

- Arrange the fixtures in attractive clusters to draw the eye to different sections of the room. The toilet and bidet comprise one distinct area, with a false half-height wall concealing the toilet cistern on a back-to-wall model.
- The half-height wall provides a useful link to the bathing area, as it can be used for bathside toiletries and accessories.
- At the other end of the room, the vanity unit basin and rectangular shower make another distinctive area. The two sections are linked by the tall freestanding towel cabinet placed between the bath and shower.

ABOVE Add a half-height wall to break up a long bathroom and provide a stylish support for a wall-hung basin.

COLOURS: Combine pretty greens and creams to create a feeling of spaciousness. Horizontal stripes in varying widths on the short end wall will help make the room seem wider.

Problem 2

This bathroom is long but also very small and lacks the space for a bath.

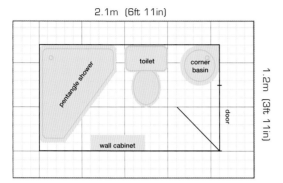

2.1m (6ft 11in)
1.2m (3ft 11in)

pentangle shower
toilet
corner basin
door
wall cabinet

Solution

- An angular shower unit draws the eye forward as soon as you step in the room and makes a feature out of the end of the room, making it seem nearer and less corridor-like. A sliding door on the shower will save room.
- A small corner basin is ideal for a tight space and allows enough room for the bathroom door to open.
- The double wall cabinet provides ample storage and breaks up the long wall. Add a few glass or mirror tiles along this wall to create extra interest. Imaginative lighting is another good way to create an interesting feature. Use medium-low wall lighting to break up a wall, or direct spotlights into dark corners or areas of activity.

COLOURS: If you are designing a small bathroom and want a splash of colour, choose chalky pastel shades that will not overpower the space.

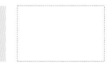

Problem 3

Again, this very narrow room will not take a bath widthways and so gives the impression of a long corridor.

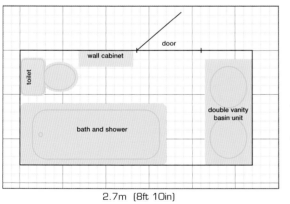

door
wall cabinet
toilet
1.3m (4ft 3in)
bath and shower
double vanity basin unit
2.7m (8ft 10in)

Solution

- Create a feature at one end of the room with a large double vanity sink unit. Add a wall cabinet for decorative interest and extra storage, or use 'floating' shelves, painted the same colour as the walls, for an alternative effect.
- Fit an over-bath shower and add a glass shower screen along the side of the bath to prevent splashes and create a private area for the toilet alongside.
- Double wall cabinets along the opposite wall break up the expanse of space. Alternatively, fit a mirror along this wall to make it seem bigger.

COLOURS: Keeping the backdrop neutral, paint a vibrant feature wall at the short end of the room in a lively citrus shade.

small bathrooms

The bathroom is often the smallest room in the house and designing a layout that is efficient, effective and appealing can pose quite a challenge. If knocking down walls is not an option, you will have to work within the size restrictions but there are a few clever tricks you can bring into play to maximize the feeling of space.

Using the right colours will really make a difference. Stick to light colours for a spacious feel as dark colours will only make the walls seem closer. Use lots of mirrors and reflective surfaces like metal, glass and chrome to reflect light and make the room seem bigger. If possible, place the mirror opposite a window for best effects.

Avoid heavy ornate designs and bulky furniture, which will make the room seem crowded and cramped. Opt for just a few small, delicately crafted accessories instead. Fixtures with curved sculptured edges will make the space seem fluid, hard edges will create a sharp angular effect. Choose fittings carefully – chrome or brass taps are good for a simple classic look, porcelain handles give a delicate impression. Choose recessed lighting rather than wall-mounted or pendant lights, which will obscure areas. Keep the space free of clutter by hiding bottles, soaps and toiletries in cabinets, or neatly grouping them on a trolley.

ABOVE Streamlined fixtures and reflective surfaces will give a really tiny bathroom a modern spacious appeal.

Problem 1

The room has a box-like shape, which can be difficult to make visually appealing.

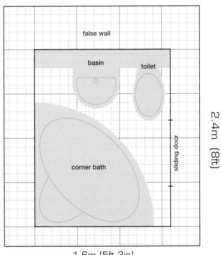

false wall

basin

toilet

sliding door

2.4m (8ft)

corner bath

1.6m (5ft 3in)

Solution

- A corner bath is not only a great space saver for a small bathroom, it also makes an interesting feature and adds a touch of luxury to what would otherwise be a tiny cramped room.
- A corner bath is also a very comfortable option for an over-bath shower and a stylish shower curtain will add texture and colour.
- The false wall, built to hide the toilet cistern, offers great storage options. It can be fitted with recessed shelving, cupboards or sliding drawers for a very neat effect. The wall-hung toilet and basin also create a neat streamlined effect and give the illusion of more space.
- A sliding door as the entrance to the bathroom makes the most of the limited space available for fixtures.

ABOVE Keep colours neutral and opt for a space-saving fixture like this luxurious corner bath to make smaller bathrooms work.

COLOURS: Neutral colours such as white, cream and stone are perfect for making small spaces appear bigger.

Problem 2

This room is too small to fit a standard bath, and normal size fixtures make the room seem very cramped.

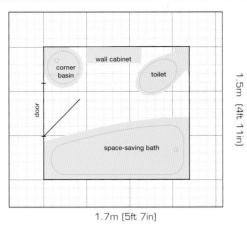

corner basin
wall cabinet
door
toilet
space-saving bath

1.5m (4ft 11in)

1.7m (5ft 7in)

ABOVE **A neat corner basin is a great space-saving idea.**

Solution

- The specially designed ergonomic bath is narrow at one end to fit neatly into a small space while still providing a generous curved area at the other end for over-bath showering. A bath that is shorter than a standard bath is ideal for the smaller bathroom.
- When space is tight, make use of even the tightest corners with corner fixtures like toilets and basins.
- Look upwards for storage. You may find you have to utilize all your floor space for fixtures in a small bathroom, so consider storage options at shoulder height or higher. A wall-hung cabinet is a good option.
- The toilet hangs on a false wall, which could also be utilized for extra storage.

COLOURS: Lilac is the perfect colour for small spaces as it is easy on the eye. Add splashes of purple for a textured look.

Problem 3

This small bathroom has the added problem of a curved wall, which cuts into the available space.

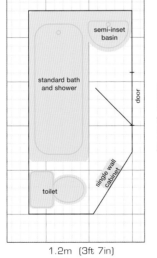

semi-inset basin
standard bath and shower
door
single wall cabinet
toilet

2.3m (7ft 7in)

1.2m (3ft 7in)

LEFT **Mirrors and reflective surfaces increase the feeling of light and space and make small bathrooms look bigger.**

Solution

- The room is large enough to take a standard bath, which can also be fitted with a shower. Adding a shower screen along one side will protect the room from splashes and also create a neat divide between the bath and sink.
- Use the curved wall space for hanging wall cabinets for storage.
- The basin is a semi-inset counter basin. This looks less bulky than a standard vanity sink in a small bathroom, but still offers valuable under-sink storage space.

COLOURS: Pale shades of blue and green are receding colours that will naturally draw out a room Use with plenty of white for a great effect.

L-shaped bathrooms

An L-shaped room can be a planning nightmare, with an awkward protrusion that detracts from the unified feel of the room. Don't despair – weigh up all the options and turn the negatives into positive features.

Make the alcove work for you. Don't try to assimilate it into the rest of the room at all costs if this simply will not work. Instead consider screening it off with a half-height wall, glass blocks or screen and using it for certain functions. Make it a dedicated wash area, a private space for the toilet or a storage and dressing area. Consider installing a streamlined corner bath to introduce soft curved lines into the room and make it look less like a hallway. Avoid angular fixtures and fittings which will make the room feel boxy.

Use accent lighting to highlight individual features and draw your eye around the room. Try a row of halogen mini lights along a recessed cabinet edge or a few spotlights over the bath. Don't let the short end of the bathroom become a dark corner – make sure it is brightly lit and create the illusion of extra height and space with halogen spotlights fitted flush to the ceiling. Clever use of mirrors will reflect light back into the room and help make it feel bigger by brightening up dark corners.

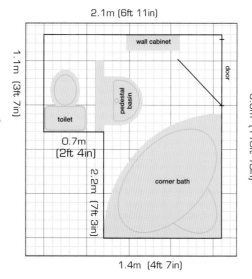

ABOVE Used cleverly, an awkward alcove can provide a private area for a toilet and bidet.

Problem 1

The room has an awkward alcove, which is not large enough to take a bath or a shower cubicle with an opening door.

Plan dimensions: 2.1m (6ft 11in) · 1.1m (3ft 7in) · wall cabinet · door · 3.3m (11ft 10in) · pedestal basin · toilet · 0.7m (2ft 4in) · 2.2m (7ft 3in) · corner bath · 1.4m (4ft 7in)

ABOVE Mount a mirror behind the basin to reflect light back into the room, helping it to feel brighter and more spacious.

Solution

• Create a private area for the toilet by building a wall to partially screen the alcove from the rest of the room. Opt for a half-height wall if you want to keep a more integrated feel within the room, or use glass bricks, an excellent way to create a secluded area without losing any light.

• The partition wall creates an ideal support for the pedestal basin. A full-height wall would also accommodate shelves or a medicine cabinet over the basin for storage. The wall clearly delineates the room into washing and toilet facilities.

• The curved corner bath at the end of the bathroom breaks up the length of the room and stops it looking like a long narrow corridor.

• There is enough space at the end of the room for a double wall cabinet.

COLOURS: Combine splashes of bright blue and yellow for a fun Mediterranean scheme that's really easy to live with.

Problem 2

The room is quite angular with a protruding end but very spacious.

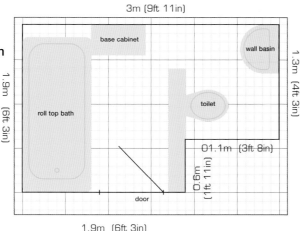

3m (9ft 11in)

base cabinet

wall basin

1.3m (4ft 3in)

1.9m (6ft 3in)

roll top bath

toilet

□1.1m (3ft 8in)

0.6m (1ft 11in)

door

1.9m (6ft 3in)

ABOVE Place the bath in a recessed area to create a relaxing retreat for bathing.

Solution

- Make the most of the positive aspects of this room. The room is large enough lengthways to take a freestanding roll top bath, which makes a stunning impact on entering the room. Build a false half-height wall to divide the awkward L-shape and create two contained areas, strategically lit with focused lighting.
- The false wall also makes it possible to fit a neat wall-hung toilet, as the cistern can be contained within it. Hang a matching basin on the opposite wall for a pleasing symmetrical and streamlined effect. Alternatively, use a traditional cistern toilet and place it parallel to the false wall for a more secluded feel.
- For added appeal, raise the flooring in the basin and toilet area to create two separate sections and give more definition to the room.

COLOURS: A combination of muted greens and white with a splash of black will create a stylish, period scheme that will open up the space in an awkwardly-shaped bathroom.

Problem 3

An L-shaped room that is too small to fit a standard sized bath.

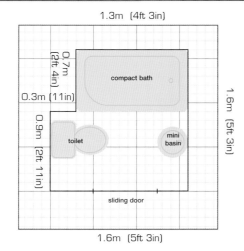

1.3m (4ft 3in)

0.7m (2ft 4in)

compact bath

0.3m (11in)

1.6m (5ft 3in)

0.9m (2ft 11in)

toilet

mini basin

sliding door

1.6m (5ft 3in)

ABOVE Place the toilet in the slightly longer end of the room. This will screen it at least partially from the bath.•

Solution

- Take advantage of the number of fixtures on the market specially designed for small or awkwardly shaped bathrooms. A compact space-saving bath is an excellent solution when space is tight, and fits neatly into the awkwardly shaped alcove in this room. The small space left at the end of the bath could be made into a shelf and tiled over for toiletries.
- A compact mini basin is ideal for a small room.
- Consider building shelving or cabinets above the bath and basin, or hanging attractive baskets or chrome wire caddies to display toiletries and rolled towels.

COLOURS: Aqua and cream will help make a bathroom appear bigger while touches of chocolate will add depth to the scheme.

awkwardly shaped bathrooms

If you have an awkwardly shaped bathroom, you will need to work extra hard to make it feel light, open and spacious. You may have to deal with low or sloping ceilings, slanting walls, lots of corners and tricky alcoves. It is a huge challenge, but the end result doesn't have to be an awkward-looking bathroom.

If you have a sloping ceiling, arrange your fixtures to suit. Place the shower and basin in the tall section of the room where you need to stand upright, and position the foot end of the bath where the ceiling is lowest or, depending on the incline, place the bath under the slope.

Make the most of the limitations. Although a sloping ceiling creates an odd-shaped room, it offers fantastic potential for natural light by fitting a skylight. A skylight lets in five times as much light as a window the same size.

Fix lights flush to the ceiling to increase the feeling of height in the room, and prevent hanging light fittings from becoming a dangerous obstruction.

Bathrooms with sloping ceilings are generally quite small. Compensate with bright soft colours, or neutral shades to open out the space. Often it can be difficult to decide where the walls end and the ceiling starts. If this is the case you may end up using the same colour on the entire room so it is very important to keep it light. Place mirrors at strategic angles to increase the perceived size of the room, or use mirrors and mirrored tiles to open up awkward recesses.

Be clever when planning and use the awkward shapes to greatest advantage. Consider fitting a large walk-in shower or built-in storage unit in a difficult corner or large recess.

ABOVE Sloping ceilings are not necessarily a drawback. With a bit of careful planning and colour scheming they can be transformed into an elegant design feature.

Problem 1

You could easily end up with this type of room after sectioning off part of a bedroom to make an en-suite bathroom. Or you might have inherited it in an old house with quirky room divisions. The room dimensions are small and its awkward shape makes it impossible to fit either a full-sized bath or shower.

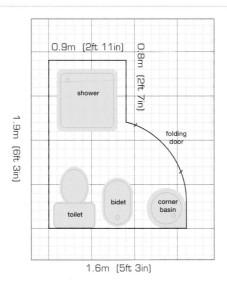

Solution

- Fit a compact shower in the recessed area. Consider using frosted glass or glass blocks to section this area off from the room next door, and allow lots of light through for a pleasant effect when showering.
- A corner basin is a compact option and accentuates the natural curve of the wall.
- Despite the room's small dimensions, careful planning means there is enough space to fit both a toilet and bidet. This is a luxurious touch if you are using this room as your main bathroom. Or you could do without the bidet and fit a larger basin instead.
- A sliding or folding door in the curved wall for entry into the room is both an excellent space-saving idea and an attractive feature in the smaller bathroom.

A B O V E Corner showers or those with sliding doors are ideal options if you are dealing with a very tight space. There are plenty of alternatives on the market.

C O L O U R S : In a confined space, stick to a neutral colour palette to make the room appear bigger.

Problem 2

You will have to deal with a sloping ceiling if you are installing a bathroom in an attic conversion. A sloping ceiling makes it awkward to position fixtures that provide the user with enough head room, while avoiding lining everything up against one wall.

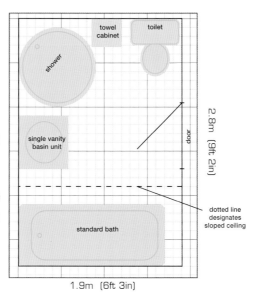

Solution

- Place the bath under the sloping ceiling, allowing it to take advantage of the natural light from a skylight by day and atmospheric star spotting by night.
- The tall part of the room is kept clear for full-height fixtures like the basin, toilet and shower. A compact circular shower cubicle fits neatly in the space.
- Place a towel cabinet close to the shower if possible.

A B O V E Wall-mounted accessories are great space-saving options in cramped bathrooms.

C O L O U R S : A clever combination of pale tones can be used on walls and ceilings to create the illusion of space and light.

quick project guide

Here is an at-a-glance guide to the projects that appear throughout this book. Simply choose one that suits your level of skill, your time-scale or your bathroom's decorative or storage needs.

Easy projects

Simple projects that are ideal for a DIY novice.

Intermediate projects

An exciting range of designs for those with a little experience.

Advanced projects

These are a bit more difficult. Read each step carefully before you begin.

Decorative Ideas

Inspiration and suggestions for a host of projects.

Storage Solutions

Not enough space? Solve your problems with one of these smart solutions.

4-hour projects

If you have more time to spare, one of these projects will easily fit into a morning or afternoon.

2-hour projects

Excellent ideas for really quick bathroom projects.

6-hour projects

These projects will take longer, but are well worth it.

1-day and 2-day projects

Transform your bathroom over a weekend.

index

index

acknowledgements

The Amtico Company Ltd. /tel: 0800 667766 /www.amtico.com 28, 124.

Armitage Shanks /tel: 01543 490 253 / www.armitage-shanks.co.uk 44 right, 104, 105, 106 left, 107 left, 108 top, 108 bottom, 109 right, 109 top left, 109 bottom left.

Christy /tel: 08457 585 252 /www.christy-towels.com 34.
Colourwash /tel: 020 8944 6456 /www.colourwash.co.uk 3 top, 18, 42.

Dolomite /tel: 0800 138 0922 /www.dolomite-bathrooms.com 12, 45, 57, 128 right.

Dolphin Bathrooms /tel: 0800 626 717/ www.dolphinbathrooms.com 6-7 centre, 40 left, 46 top left, 46 bottom left, 46-47.

Dulux /tel: 01753 550 555 /www.dulux.co.uk 26 left.

Fired Earth /tel: 01295 814 300 /www.firedearth.com 21 left, 38, 129 top.

Graham Brown /tel: 0800 328 8452 /www.grahambrown.com 32.

H&R Johnson Tiles /tel: 01782 575 575 /www.johnson-tiles.com 10.

The Holding Company /tel: 020 8445 2888 / www.theholdingcompany.co.uk 11, 51, 100.

www.homebase.co.uk 1, 2, 3 bottom, 14 left, 16, 17, 19, 20, 21 right, 22, 23, 24 centre left, 24 bottom, 33 bottom, 35 left, 48 left, 48 right, 50, 52 left, 55, 58 top, 60-61, 62, 63, 64 left, 64 top right, 64 bottom right, 65 left, 65 centre right, 65 bottom right, 65 bottom centre, 66 left, 66 top right, 66 bottom right, 67 right, 67 top left, 67 bottom left, 68, 69, 70 left, 70 centre right, 70 bottom right, 71, 71 centre right, 71 bottom right, 71 bottom centre, 72 left, 72 top right, 73 top left, 73 top right, 73 bottom, 74, 75, 76 left, 76 top right, 76 bottom right, 77 left, 77 bottom right, 77 centre right, 78 left, 78 top right, 78 bottom right, 79 top left, 79 top right, 79 bottom, 80, 81, 82, 83, 84 top, 84 bottom, 85 right, 85 top left, 85 bottom left, 86, 87, 88 left, 88 right, 89, 90 left, 90 top right, 90 bottom right, 91 top left, 91 top right, 91 bottom, 92, 93, 94, 95, 96 left, 96 right, 97 top, 97 bottom right, 97 bottom left, 101, 106 right, 107 right, 112 right, 113 right, 116, 117, 118 left, 118 top right, 118 bottom right, 119 left, 119 top right, 119 bottom right, 120 left, 120 top right, 120 bottom right, 121 top, 121 bottom right, 121 bottom left, 128 left, 131 top, 132 right, 133 top, 133 bottom.

Ideal Standard Ltd /tel: 01482 346 461/ www.ideal-standard.co.uk 5 right, 7 right, 13, 14 right, 15, 26 right, 29, 30, 39 top, 40 top right, 41 right, 43 left, 43 right, 49, 56, 58 left, 122-123, 130 right, 130 top left, 132 top, 135 bottom, 137 top.

International Paints /tel: 01962 717 001/ www.international-paints.co.uk 27.

Royal Doulton Bathrooms /tel: 0870 241 4456 / www.royaldoultonbathroooms.com 5 left, 25, 33 top, 44 left, 54, 134 top.

Twyford Bathrooms /tel: 0870 242 2440/ www.twyfordbathrooms.com 35 right, 39 bottom, 59, 131 bottom, 134 right, 135, 135 top, 136.

Vitra /tel: 01235 820 400. 4, 8-9, 37, 41 left, 52-53 centre, 58 bottom right, 124-125, 129 bottom, 137 bottom.

Wickes Building Supplies Ltd. /tel: 0500 300 328/ www.wickes.co.uk 98, 99, 102 left, 102 top right, 102 centre right, 103 left, 103 right, 110, 111, 112 left, 113 left, 114 left, 114 top right, 114 bottom right, 115 top, 115 bottom right, 115 bottom left.

acknowledgements

Authors' acknowledgements

We would like to thank all of the people involved in the creation of this book, and all of the people who gave their help and support to aid its completion.

A very special thanks to Lauren Floodgate and Karen O'Grady or their invaluable comments, advice and suggestions at every stage of the project.

Thank you also to the photographers: Graham Ainscogh, Lucy Pope and Howard Shooter; and the stylists: Jane Davies and Nancy Hamilton.

Thanks to the companies who gave practical advice and supplied imagery to aid in the production of this book.

A final thanks has to go to editors Jennifer Mussett, Doreen Palamartschuk-Gillon and Clare Churly at Hamlyn for their continuous enthusiasm and ongoing support throughout the project.

Executive Editor Doreen Palamartschuk-Gillon
Managing Editor Clare Churly
Executive Art Editor Joanna Bennett
Designer Ruth Hope
Picture Researcher Zoë Holtermann
Senior Production Controller Louise Hall

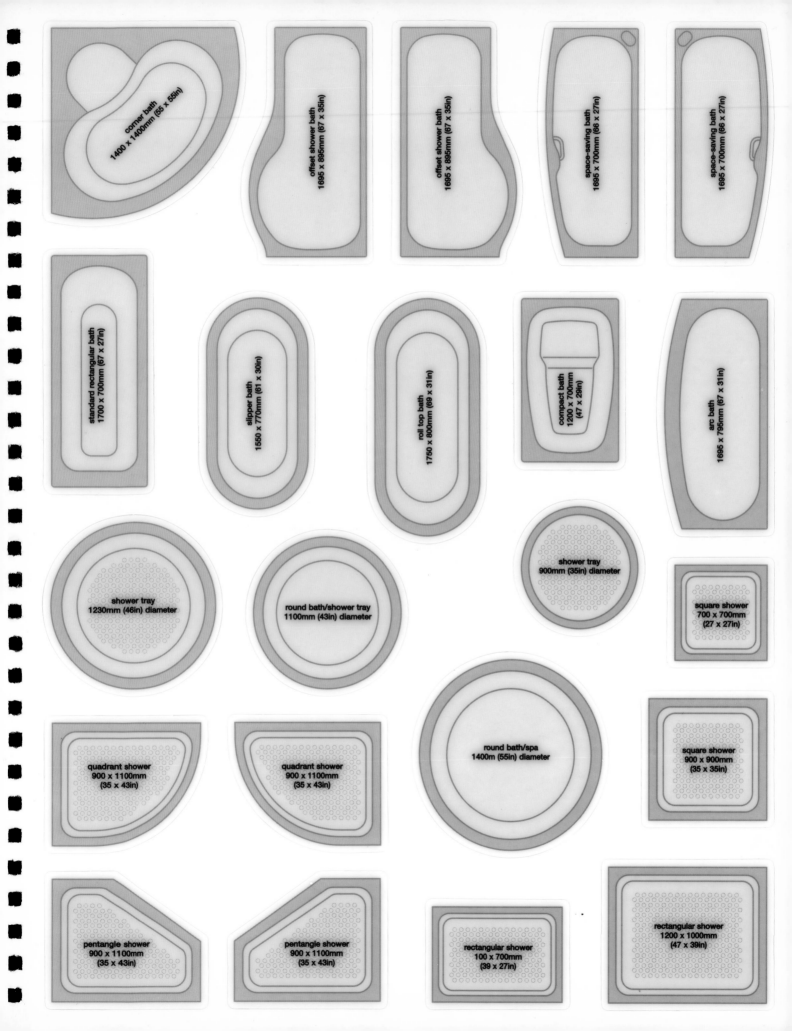

corner bath
1400 x 1400mm (55 x 55in)

offset shower bath
1695 x 895mm (67 x 35in)

offset shower bath
1695 x 895mm (67 x 35in)

space-saving bath
1695 x 700mm (66 x 27in)

space-saving bath
1695 x 700mm (66 x 27in)

standard rectangular bath
1700 x 700mm (67 x 27in)

slipper bath
1550 x 770mm (61 x 30in)

roll top bath
1750 x 800mm (69 x 31in)

compact bath
1200 x 700mm
(47 x 29in)

arc bath
1695 x 795mm (67 x 31in)

shower tray
1230mm (46in) diameter

round bath/shower tray
1100mm (43in) diameter

shower tray
900mm (35in) diameter

square shower
700 x 700mm
(27 x 27in)

quadrant shower
900 x 1100mm
(35 x 43in)

quadrant shower
900 x 1100mm
(35 x 43in)

round bath/spa
1400m (55in) diameter

square shower
900 x 900mm
(35 x 35in)

pentangle shower
900 x 1100mm
(35 x 43in)

pentangle shower
900 x 1100mm
(35 x 43in)

rectangular shower
100 x 700mm
(39 x 27in)

rectangular shower
1200 x 1000mm
(47 x 39in)

rectangular basin
600 x 550mm
(24 x 21in)

double basin
1200 x 560mm (47 x 22in)

single vanity
1000 x 560mm
(39 x 22in)

single vanity
600 x 585mm
(24 x 23in)

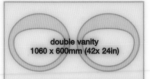
double vanity
1060 x 600mm (42 x 24in)

rectangular basin
600 x 550mm
(24 x 21in)

double basin
1200 x 560mm (47 x 22in)

single vanity
1000 x 560mm
(39 x 22in)

single vanity
600 x 585mm
(24 x 23in)

double vanity
1060 x 600mm (42x 24in)

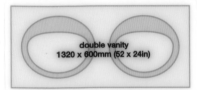
double vanity
1320 x 600mm (52 x 24in)

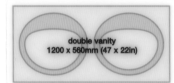
double vanity
1250 x 560mm 49 x 22"

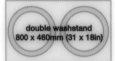
double vanity
1200 x 560mm (47 x 22in)

double washstand
800 x 460mm (31 x 18in)

double vanity
1320 x 600mm (52 x 24in)

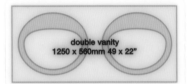
double vanity
1250 x 560mm (49 x 22in)

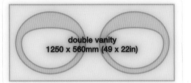
double vanity
1200 x 560mm (47 x 22in)

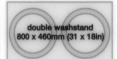
double washstand
800 x 460mm (31 x 18in)

basin
360mm
(14in)
diameter

basin
360mm
(14in)
diameter

handbasin
350 x 250mm
(14 x 10in)

handbasin
460 x 360mm
(18 x 14in)

pedestal basin
560 x 460mm
(22 x 18in)

pedestal basin
560 x 460mm
(22 x 18in)

short-projection
basin
560 x 360mm
(22 x 14in)

corner basin
460 x 460mm
(18 x 18in)

wallmounted
bidet
560 x 380mm
(22 x 15in)

floorstanding
bidet
600 x 380mm
(24 x 15in)

back-to-wall
bidet
600 x 380mm
(24 x 15in)

semi-countertop
basin
560 x 460mm
(22 x 18in)

semi-countertop
basin
560 x 460mm
(22 x 18in)

narrow basin
450 x 500mm
(18 x 20in)

corner basin
460 x 460mm
(18 x 18in)

corner basin
460 x 460mm
(18 x 18in)

back-to-wall
bidet
569 x 360mm
(22 x 14in)

wall mounted
bidet
600 x 380mm
(24 x 15in)

floor-standing
bidet
560 x 360mm
(22 x 14in)

back-to-wall
toilet
500 x 360mm
(20 x 14in)

wall mounted
toilet
600 x 380mm
(24 x 15in)

close coupled
toilet

675 x 425mm
(26 x 17in)

close-coupled
toilet

700 x 520mm
(27 x 13in)

narrow toilet
640 x 365mm
(25 x 14in)

double base cabinet
640 x 350mm
(25 x 13in)

double base cabinet
640 x 350mm
(25 x 13in)

single base
cabinet
320 x 350mm
12 x 13"

single base
cabinet
320 x 350mm
12 x 13"

single base
cabinet
320 x 280mm
(12 x 11in)

single base
cabinet
320 x 280mm
(12 x 11in)

corner toilet
385 x 730mm
(29 x 15in)

low-level
toilet

700 x 500mm
(27 x 20in)

double base cabinet
640 x 280mm
(25 x 11in)

double base cabinet
640 x 280mm
(25 x 11in)

wall cabinet
320 x 180mm
(12 x 7in)

wall cabinet
320 x 180mm
(12 x 7in)

double wall cabinet
640 x 180mm
(25 x 7in)

double wall cabinet
640 x 180mm
(25 x 7in)

corner
cabinet
230 x 230mm
(9 x 9in)

corner
cabinet
230 x 230mm
(9 x 9in)

corner
cabinet
400 x 400mm
(16 x 16in)

corner
cabinet
400 x 400mm
(16 x 16in)

corner
cabinet
350 x 350mm
(13 x 13in)

corner
cabinet
350 x 350mm
(13 x 13in)

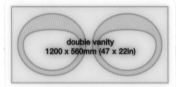